Level 2 Diploma for IT Users
for City & Guilds

Word Processing

for Office XP

Level

2

Rosemarie Wyatt

Endorsed by

**City&
Guilds**

www.heinemann.co.uk
✓ Free online support
✓ Useful weblinks
✓ 24 hour online ordering

01865 888058

Heinemann
Inspiring generations

Heinemann Educational Publishers
Halley Court, Jordan Hill, Oxford OX2 8EJ
Part of Harcourt Education

Heinemann is the registered trademark of
Harcourt Education Limited

© Rosemarie Wyatt, 2004

First published 2004

09 08 07 06
10 9 8 7 6 5 4 3 2

British Library Cataloguing in Publication Data is available
from the British Library on request.

10-digit ISBN: 0 435462 53 9
13-digit ISBN: 978 0 435462 53 6

Publisher's note
The materials in this Work have been developed by Harcourt Education and the
content and the accuracy are the sole responsibility of Harcourt Education. The City
and Guilds of London Institute accepts no liability howsoever in respect of any
breach of the intellectual property rights of any third party howsoever occasioned or
damage to the third party's property or person as a result of the use of this Work.

The City & Guilds name and logo are the registered trade marks of The City and
Guilds of London Institute and are used under licence.

Typeset by Tech-Set Ltd, Gateshead, Tyne and Wear
Printed in the UK by Thomson Litho Ltd.

Acknowledgements
The publishers wish to acknowledge that the screenshots in this book have been
reprinted with kind permission from Microsoft Corporation.

Tel: 01865 888058 www.heinemann.co.uk

Contents

Introduction

City & Guilds e-Quals is an exciting new range of IT qualifications developed with leading industry experts. These comprehensive, progressive awards cover everything from getting to grips with basic IT to gaining the latest professional skills.

The range consists of both User and Practitioner qualifications. User qualifications (Levels 1–3) are ideal for those who use IT as part of their job or in life generally, while Practitioner qualifications (Levels 2–3) have been developed for those who need to boost their professional skills in, for example, networking or software development.

e-Quals boasts online testing and a dedicated website with news and support materials and web-based training. The qualifications reflect industry standards and meet the requirements of the National Qualifications Framework. With e-Quals you will not only develop your expertise, you will gain a qualification that is recognised by employers all over the world.

This book assumes that you have acquired the skills and knowledge necessary for Word Processing Level 2 and builds on those skills, introducing additional features such as styles, templates and mail merge.

The unit is organised into 6 outcomes. You will learn to:
- Plan and prepare to produce new documents
- Produce new documents
- Produce new documents using mail merge facilities
- Edit existing documents
- Check produced documents
- Save and print documents

The specific skills and underpinning knowledge for the outcomes of this Word Processing unit are covered, although they are not dealt with separately or in the same order.

Each section covers several practical skills as well as underpinning knowledge related to the unit outcomes. This is followed by skills practice and a chance to check your knowledge. Consolidation tasks give you the opportunity to put together skills and knowledge, and a practice assignment completes your progress towards the actual assignment. Solutions can be found at the back of the book.

Your tutor will give you a copy of the outcomes, as provided by City & Guilds, so that you can sign and date each learning point as you master the skills and knowledge.

In order to give detailed methods for each task it is necessary to refer to a specific word processing application and operating system, though the City & Guilds unit is not specific and can be completed using any word processing application and operating system. This book refers to Microsoft Word for Office XP.

There is often more than one way of carrying out a task in Word, e.g. using the toolbar, menu or keyboard. Whilst this book may use one method, there are others, and alternatives are listed at the back in the quick reference guide.

The tasks are designed to be worked through in order, as earlier tasks may be used in later sections. Good luck!

You will learn to

- Revise basics – enter text, edit, format, save, print
- Revise cut, copy and paste text

This book assumes that you have already acquired the skills and knowledge for Word Processing Level 1, and as those topics will be familiar to you, you may be given brief reminders rather than full instructions. The Check your knowledge at the end of this section, and others, includes questions that test knowledge required for Level 2 previously covered in Level 1. This will provide useful revision.

You should already be able to:

- Enter and edit text (insert and delete)
- Format text (change font, size, emphasis, alignment)
- Select paper size, orientation and margins
- Save and print
- Use Save As
- Cut and paste
- Consider the use of fonts

Information

Documents created in this section and others will be used in later sections. Do not omit tasks.

Hint:

The term **document** generally relates to word processed materials whereas the term **file** can be used for other types as well, e.g. spreadsheets. The two terms are interchangeable throughout this book.

Remember:

One space after a comma. One or two spaces at the end of a sentence after a full stop, ? or ! but be consistent.
One space before and after a dash used as a pause – as used here.
No spaces before and after a hyphen linking two words together, e.g. well-known.

| Task 1.1 | Revise basics |

Method

1. Load Word. A new blank document should appear. If not, click on the **File** menu and select **New**.
2. Key in the following text.

Team working

A group of people working well together will usually complete a task quicker than one person on their own. There is a well-known saying – many hands make light work – and another similar one – two heads are better than one. However, it is not quite as simple as that as successful team working depends on a number of factors.

If a group of people are put together as a team to work on a project, they may have no idea how to begin. In a small team there may be no appointed leader, but often a natural leader will emerge. If there is a leader the team will look to the leader to get things started. As the

team members begin to work together, progress can be made. If they do not co-operate and work well together then progress will be difficult. Problems can occur if everyone does not pull their weight or if some people feel their contribution is not valued by others.

3   Spellcheck and proofread.

4   Click on **Save** and key in the filename **Teamworking**.

5   Click on **Print**

6   Select the **File** menu, choose **Page Setup** and click on the **Margins** tab (Figure 1.1).

7   Click on **landscape** orientation and key in **3** in the **Top** margin box. Repeat for the **Bottom**, **Left** and **Right**.

8   Click on the **Paper** tab and from the drop down arrow by **Paper size**, select A5.

9   Click **OK**.

Information: Revise page size and formatting

Paper size

The standard size used for printers and photocopiers is **A4** (the size of pages in this book). This is based on International Standard (ISO) sizes where each size is half that of the next biggest size.

A3	A4	A5	A6
297 × 420 mm	210 × 297 mm	148 × 210 mm	105 × 148 mm

Generally, all printers take A4 paper and most will handle smaller sizes. Those that accept A3 paper are less common and anything bigger than A3 would require specialist printing.

Typical uses

A3	Drawings, diagrams, posters
A4	Letters, memos, advertising flyers, forms, reports, booklets, newsletters
A5	Memos, advertising flyers, booklets, forms, notepads
A6	Postcards, invitations, notepads, advertisements
Custom size	You can also set a page up with your own chosen measurements for any purpose.

Page orientation

A page can be set up as either portrait (tall) or landscape (wide). Most documents on A4 will use portrait orientation.

Short edge at the top

Short edge at the side

Portrait   Landscape

Formatting

Formatting means to change the appearance of a document. **Page formatting** may involve changing the size and orientation of the page and/or the margins – the space between the text and the edge of the page. Both can be changed by selecting **Page Setup** from the **File** menu.

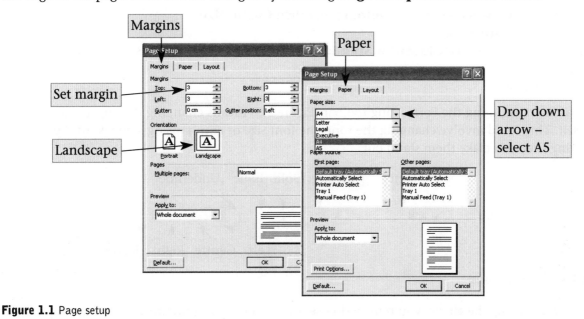

Figure 1.1 Page setup

Information: The Task pane

The Task pane appears on the right hand side of the screen. This is available for many different tasks. It opens automatically when you start a task for which a pane exists. It can be opened and closed as required. To open it select **Task pane** from the **View** menu.

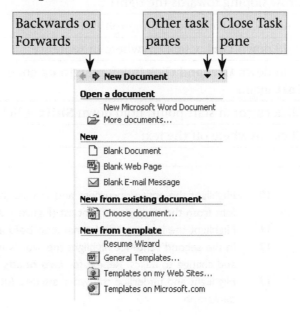

Figure 1.2 Task pane

Information: Revise text formatting and selecting text

For the purpose of this book it would be helpful to see both the full **Standard** and **Formatting** toolbars. If both are not fully displayed, do this now:

- Click on the **View** menu, select **Toolbars** and then **Customize**.
- Click on the **Options** tab.
- Click in the check box labelled **Show Standard and Formatting toolbars on two rows** to put a tick in it.
- Click on **Close**.

Text formatting using the Formatting toolbar (Figure 1.3) means changing the appearance of the text itself. This could involve changing the font, the font size or emphasising some words by enhancing them, to make them stand out.

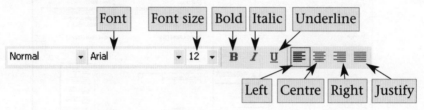

Figure 1.3 Formatting toolbar

To format text using the above, you must either select the text by highlighting it after keying it in, or choose the required formatting beforehand. Try these methods of selecting text now.

To select:	Method
One word	Double click on word (also selects the following space)
Several words	Press and drag the I-beam across several words and release
A line	Click alongside a line in the left margin (mouse pointer changes to an arrow sloping towards the right)
A paragraph	Double click alongside paragraph in left margin
A sentence	Hold down **Ctrl**. Click anywhere in sentence
Whole document	Hold down **Ctrl** and click in left margin **or** choose **Select All** from the **Edit** menu.
A block of text	Click cursor at start point, hold down **Shift**. Click cursor at end point
To deselect	Click anywhere off the text

10 Highlight the entire document and change the font to **Arial** by selecting the font from the drop down font list (Figure 1.3).
11 Highlight the heading and format it to **bold** and size **14**.
12 In the second sentence highlight the words **many hands make light work** and change to italics. Repeat for **two heads are better than one**.
13 Highlight and underline the word **successful** in the last sentence of the first paragraph.

Information: Revise alignment

Left align Each line starts at the left margin. Considered to be the easiest alignment to read. (Also known as left justified or ragged right, as each line ends at a different point.)
Justify A straight left and right margin.
Centre Text centred between the margins.
Right align Each line ends at the right margin. Probably the least used alignment.

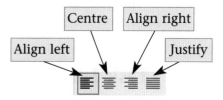

Figure 1.4 Alignment

Alignment can be changed by selecting the text by highlighting it after keying it in, or by choosing the required alignment beforehand.

14   Centre the heading and **justify** the two paragraphs.
15   Insert your name as a **footer**. (Select **View** menu – **Header and Footer** – click on **Switch between Header and Footer** .) If you cannot remember how to do this, leave it out for now – this topic is fully covered in the next section.
16   Save and print.

Information: Revise editing

Editing means to change the content of a document, particularly the text. It might involve deleting words, inserting words, joining and splitting paragraphs. It also includes moving text around as well as images and other objects, such as charts.

17   In the first sentence of the first paragraph, delete the word **usually** and insert **generally** in its place.
18   Join the two paragraphs together. (Position cursor at the end of the first paragraph and press **Delete** twice on the keyboard.) Ensure one or two spaces are left between the two sentences.
19   Create a new paragraph starting with the sentence **As the team ...** (Position cursor at the start of the sentence and press **Enter** twice.)
20   Save the file with the new name – **Teamworking 2**. (Select **File** menu – **Save As** – key in the new name.)
21   Print and close the file.
22   Select **Exit** from the **File** menu to close down Word.

Remember:
Header text appears at the top of every page, and footer text at the bottom.

Remember:
When you save a file that has already been saved, the new version will replace the old one.

Remember:
Do not forget to check with your tutor about printing on A5.

Remember:
Leave one or two spaces between sentences, but always be consistent throughout.

Remember:
Save As allows you to save a file with a new name, but keeping the original intact so you have two versions. It also allows you to save a file to a different location, e.g. another folder, or to a floppy disk.

Information: Revise cut, copy and paste

Cut, copy and paste are also editing techniques. **Copying and pasting** a section of text leaves the original in place and allows you to paste a copy of it into a new position, within the same document or into another document. **Cut and paste** means that you take it from its original position, and move it to a new position.

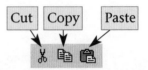

Figure 1.5 Cut, copy and paste

Task 1.2   Revise – Cut and paste text

Method

1. Load Word and a new file.
2. Key in the following text:

   Starting out

   The first thing the team must do is to ensure they know what is required of them.

   At an early stage the project must be broken down into smaller tasks and arranged to be completed in the right order with realistic deadlines. This will form the project plan. Some 'slack' should be built into the plan to allow for any problems.

   A first meeting may be a brainstorming session when team members spark ideas off each other. Some people may be good at coming up with ideas but not so good at knowing how to carry them out, whereas others do not have ideas but are very practical.

   Tasks should be shared among the team members taking into account the fact that each person is likely to have their own area of expertise and particular skills. Everyone on the team must be fully aware of their own individual responsibilities and of the deadline for their part of the project.

   It is very important that regular progress meetings are held for the whole team as this will help to ensure that deadlines are being met. It also gives the opportunity for any problems to be shared and overcome. A record of these meetings should be kept and circulated to all team members to avoid any misunderstandings.

3. Proofread and spellcheck.
4. Save as **Starting Out** and print.
5. Move the paragraph beginning **At an early stage . . .** so it becomes the third paragraph. Highlight it, including the line space below it (Figure 1.6).

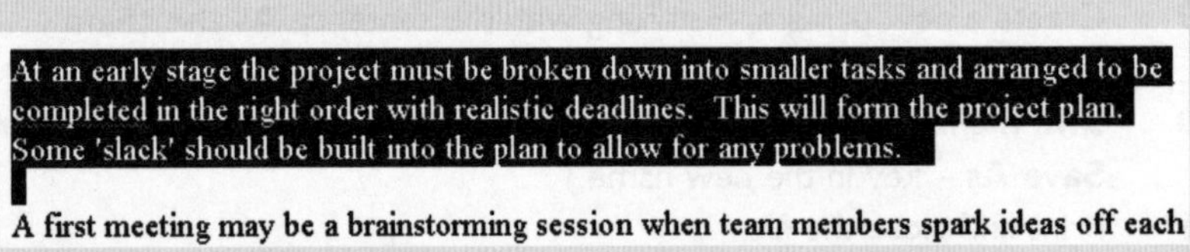

   At an early stage the project must be broken down into smaller tasks and arranged to be completed in the right order with realistic deadlines. This will form the project plan. Some 'slack' should be built into the plan to allow for any problems.

   A first meeting may be a brainstorming session when team members spark ideas off each

   Figure 1.6 Highlight text to cut

6. Click on **Cut** ✂ (Figure 1.5).
7. Move the cursor directly in front of and to the left of the first word of the paragraph beginning **Tasks . . . .**
8. Click on **Paste** 📋
9. Save the document, print and close.
10. Close Word by selecting **Exit** from the **File** menu.

Hint:

Including the space below the paragraph when highlighting means you do not have to adjust the spacing between paragraphs after moving the text.

Information: Revise fonts – style and size

Whilst this topic is covered fully in Level 1, it is important and should be revisited.

There is a huge variety of different fonts available to you. In the tasks above, you used two different fonts, **Times New Roman** (if this was your default font), which is a **serif** font, and **Arial**, which is **sans serif**. Serif fonts have small strokes at the ends of a letter, whilst sans serif fonts do not. A serif font is considered to be easier to read when used for long documents. Both of the fonts mentioned are widely used for business purposes. Depending on the document you are preparing you should choose your font carefully, as different fonts convey different meanings. For instance, you would not send a letter applying for a job using stylised fonts such as *Jokerman* or 𝕾𝕴𝕲𝕲𝖄.

The choice of font styles and sizes can have a major effect on the appearance and impact of a document, so bear the following points in mind:

- Ensure the font is appropriate for the document and will convey the right message.
- For standard business documents, Times New Roman and Arial (or similar) are considered 'safe'.
- As a general rule never use more than two fonts, or three at the most, in a document. Exceptions might be promotional material, which may particularly demand it.
- For normal continuous text, use size 10 or 12. Text below size 10 makes it difficult to read and above 12 is generally reserved for text emphasis, such as headings, or display purposes.
- Avoid too much emphasis and certainly too many different types of emphasis in one document.
- Use font style and size to give structure to a page by making main headings bigger than subheadings, which in turn should be bolder and possibly bigger than the main body of text.
- Ensure the document is legible.
- Consider house-style if appropriate. Most organisations have a house-style that sets out which font/s and sizes should be used, ensuring consistency across all their documents.

Things to do

1 Open a new file and create a list of some of the fonts available to you. Format the list so that the actual fonts are displayed. Save the file with a suitable name and print it for reference.

2 Create a new file and key in the following list:

A wedding invitation
A business letter
A children's party invitation
An advertisement for the opening of a modern art gallery
A poster advertising a murder mystery weekend
A theatre programme
Notices for a do-it-yourself shop

Select a font that would be suitable for each of the documents described and format the text using that font. Key in the name of the font used in brackets at the end of each line. Save it with a suitable name and print.

→

3   For this unit you are required to be able to identify a variety of different documents just as you did for Level 1. You should gather as many different documents as you can, e.g. letters, memos, fax cover sheets, reports, newsletter, promotional material such as advertisements and flyers, invoices, travel itineraries. Ask your friends and family if they have examples they would be willing to pass on to you. Lots of junk mail comes through your door every week by post and from advertising material inside magazines. Keep a selection.

Task 1.3   Use custom size and select fonts

In this task you will create a custom size page to produce a ticket for a quiz evening at a local school.

Method

1   Open a new document, select **Page Setup** from the **File** menu and click on the **Paper** tab (Figure 1.1).
2   Key 14 in the **Width** box and 10 in the **Height** box. Notice how the paper size changes to **Custom** size.
3   Click on the **Margins** tab (Figure 1.1).
4   Change the **Top**, **Bottom**, **Left** and **Right** margins to **2.5 cm**. Click OK.
5   Key in the following text:
    Parkway School Quiz Evening (press **Enter**)
    Friday 28th March (press **Enter**)
    7.30 pm–10 pm Doors open at 7 pm
    Tickets £5.00 (includes Ploughmans supper)
6   Centre the text and select one font and a suitable size for each line, ensuring the text remains on one page.
7   Check, save as **Quiz Ticket**, print and close.

Hint:

Some printers will not be able to accept very small sizes of paper.
Documents like tickets will often be printed with several on one page.

→ Practise your skills 1.1

1   Load Word and a new document and key in the following:

The Team
There are sometimes difficulties with team working, especially when team members do not get on, or they do not feel valued or listened to.

Team members will usually have a mixture of different personal qualities, experience, skills and knowledge and may have been picked for the team for these reasons.

Sometimes people do not pull their weight and are only too happy to sit back and let others carry them. Sometimes people will only do what they want to do. The team leader and the rest of the team have to cope with these situations. It is essential that everyone knows what is going on, what has to be done and by when. It is no good people going off in their own direction and failing to meet their targets which will then have a knock-on effect on everybody else and on the project as a whole.

2   Proofread and spellcheck.
3   Change the font throughout to a **sans serif** font.
4   Centre the heading, increase the size to **14** and **embolden** it.
5   **Justify** the three paragraphs.

6 In the first paragraph delete the words **are sometimes...** and insert the words **can be**.

7 Move the first paragraph beginning **There are sometimes...** so that it becomes the second paragraph.

8 Join the second and last paragraphs together ensuring a character space is left between them.

9 In the last paragraph, start a new paragraph beginning **It is no good...**.

10 In the third sentence of the second paragraph, change the first word **Sometimes** to **Occasionally**.

11 Change the page setup to **A5 landscape** with margins all round of **3 cm**.

12 Add a footer displaying your name. (If you cannot remember how to do this leave it out for now.)

13 Save as **The Team**, print and close.

→ Practise your skills 1.2

1 Open a new file and key in the following text:

WHAT IS A CONSERVATORY?

Once upon a time a conservatory was a glasshouse where delicate plants were placed over the winter. It was also a place where our wealthy Edwardian ancestors grew more exotic flowers and fruits than the British climate would normally allow, for example oranges – hence the term 'orangery' or the French 'orangerie'. The Crystal Palace built in Hyde Park, London, in 1851 for the Great Exhibition, was a huge conservatory consisting of over a million feet of glass. Over 6 million visitors, including many from Europe, viewed an exhibition with exhibits from all over the world. The building was divided into a series of courts featuring architecture, art, industry and nature. A circus and concerts were held within the building.

When the Great Exhibition finished, the Crystal Palace was moved to South London and rebuilt, where it remained until it was burnt down in 1936.

2 Proofread and spellcheck.

3 Save the file as **Conservatory**.

4 Change the font to a serif font of your choice making sure the text is readable.

5 Embolden the heading and change the font size to **16**.

6 Centre the heading and justify the rest of the text.

7 Make a new paragraph beginning **The Crystal Palace...**

8 Move the sentence beginning **Over 6 million visitors...** so that it becomes the last sentence of the second paragraph.

9 Join the second and third paragraphs together ensuring a space is left between sentences.

10 Insert the following sentence at the end of the first paragraph:

Many historic houses such as Blenheim Palace feature an orangery.

11 In the first sentence delete the word **over** and replace it with **for**.

12 In the third sentence of the second paragraph, insert the word **major** in front of **concerts**.

Hint:

Leave one space either side of a dash – as here, but no spaces either side of hyphen, e.g. ice-cream.

Remember:

Check carefully against the original, particularly any unusual words, proper names and numbers.

13 Change the page setup to **A5 portrait** with margins all round of **2.5 cm**.

14 Spellcheck and proofread again.

15 Add your name as a header.

16 Save the file as **Conservatory**, print and close.

Information

Some of the following questions test knowledge covered in Word Processing Level 1 that is also required for Level 2. Check your answers with the solutions provided at the back of the book and if your answers are wrong or incomplete, read the solutions carefully and then retest yourself. This applies to all sections of the book. If necessary refer back to the appropriate section in Word Processing Level 1 for further revision.

It is assumed that the Help Office Assistant is turned off. If it is on, some screen prompts may be different to those shown. See the quick reference guide at the back of this book for further guidance on Help.

→ Check your knowledge

1 What paper size and orientation are the pages of this book?

2 What is formatting?

3 What is editing?

4 What is the purpose of text enhancement and when would you use it?

5 What is justified alignment?

6 What size font and alignment is considered best for readability?

7 What is the difference between Save and Save As?

8 What is the difference between serif and sans serif fonts?

9 Name two fonts suitable for business documents.

10 Make a list of all the things you should consider when formatting text and consider font, size, emphasis and alignment.

Handling multiple documents and pages

You will learn to

- Copy and paste between documents
- Create headers and footers with appropriate content
- Use different page views
- Insert page breaks

When word processing you may often work with more than one document open at a time and with documents that consist of more than one page. In this section you will deal with copying text between files and creating headers and footers that provide useful information for the author and the end user. You should be familiar with these features in principle from Level 1.

Task 2.1	Copy and paste text between files

Method

1   Choose **Open** from the **File** menu and select **Starting Out** to open it.
2   Open the file **Teamworking 2**.
3   Open a new blank document. You should now have three documents open, one behind the other.
4   Click on the **Window** menu to see a list of the open files (Figure 2.1). The tick indicates which document is visible, i.e. on 'top' of the pile. Click on **Starting Out** to make it visible.
5   Click on the **Window** menu again, and then on **Document 1** (the blank document).
6   Key in the heading **Working in Teams** and press **Enter** twice.
7   Click on the **Window** menu and select the file **Teamworking 2**.
8   Highlight all text but not the heading.
9   Click on **Copy** 📋

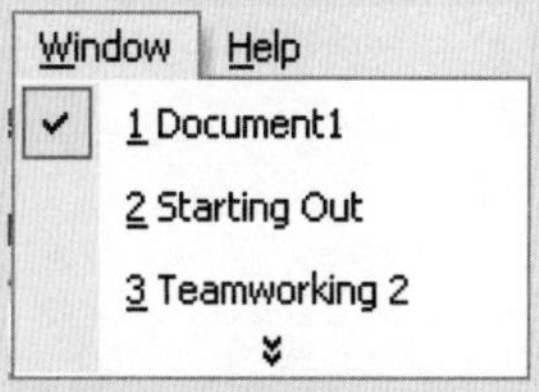

Figure 2.1 Window menu

10   Click on the **Window** menu and return to **Document 1**.
11   The cursor should be flashing in the space below the heading leaving a blank line. Click on **Paste** 📋
12   With the cursor at the end of the last paragraph, press **Enter** twice.
13   Click on the **Window** menu and select the file **Starting Out**.
14   Highlight all text including the heading and click on **Copy** 📋
15   Click on the **Window** menu and return to **Document 1**.
16   The cursor should be flashing below the last paragraph leaving a blank line. Click on **Paste** 📋
17   Adjust the line spacing if necessary.
18   Proofread, checking spacing between paragraphs is correct.

19	Save as **Working in Teams**.
20	Close the files **Starting Out** and **Teamworking 2**.
21	Open the file **The Team** and highlight all the text including the heading. Click on **Copy** 🖹
22	Click on the **Window** menu and return to **Working in Teams**.
23	Position the cursor at the end of the last paragraph and press **Enter** twice.
24	Click on **Paste** 🖺. Look in the status bar at the bottom of the screen and notice how there are now two pages (Figure 2.2).

> | Page 1 | Sec 1 | 1/2 |

Figure 2.2 Status bar

25	As the original documents were formatted differently, highlight the entire document and change the font to **Times New Roman**, size **12** with **left** alignment.
26	Embolden the headings, making the main heading size **16**.
27	Change the page margins to **3 cm** all round.
28	Save the file, print and close.

Information: Headers and footers

Headers are pieces of information that appear at the top of every page of a document. Footers appear at the bottom. They are used not only for inserting text, but also for automatic inclusion of data, such as page numbers, dates, the time and filenames. You would not normally insert a page number on a single page document but it would be usual to do so if you have more than one page. Page numbers enable the reader to follow the sequence in logical order, especially if the order becomes mixed up. They also serve as a point of reference, e.g. 'see page 6'. It is helpful if the reader knows the total number of pages they should have so they know the document is complete, e.g. Page 3 of 4. Inserting the date can be useful so the reader knows when the document was prepared, particularly when there is more than one version of it. The filename is helpful because, should you be looking at a printout some time later, it helps you to locate a file if you need to – after all, do you remember all the names of your files?

Task 2.2 | Insert a header and a footer

Method

1	Open the file **Working in Teams**.
2	Save it using **File** menu – **Save as** and the filename **Working in Teams 2**.
3	Select **View** menu – **Header and Footer**. The header area appears at the top of the page with the cursor flashing inside it (Figure 2.3). Key in your name. Notice how the text on the page below it is grey or dimmed.

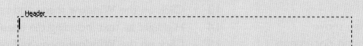

Figure 2.3 Header area

| 4 | The Header and Footer toolbar has also appeared – see Figure 2.4. Click on **Switch between Header and Footer** 🗐 |

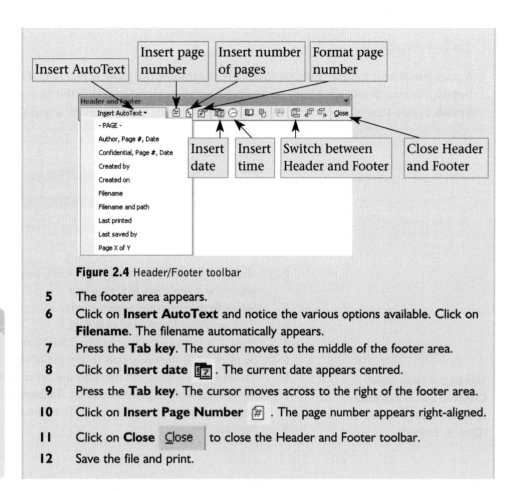

Figure 2.4 Header/Footer toolbar

5   The footer area appears.

6   Click on **Insert AutoText** and notice the various options available. Click on **Filename**. The filename automatically appears.

7   Press the **Tab key**. The cursor moves to the middle of the footer area.

8   Click on **Insert date** 🗓. The current date appears centred.

9   Press the **Tab key**. The cursor moves across to the right of the footer area.

10   Click on **Insert Page Number** # . The page number appears right-aligned.

11   Click on **Close** Close to close the Header and Footer toolbar.

12   Save the file and print.

Hint:

The Tab key is to the left of the keyboard above

Caps Lock

A tab marker is set in the middle of a header or footer and on the right.

Information: Fields

The pieces of information, such as the date and page number, that Word has inserted for you are called **fields**. Fields are placeholders for data that might change in a document. For example, if the number of pages increases, then Page 2 of 4 would become Page 2 of 5. Similarly, if the date should change, i.e. you open up a file today that you created a few days ago, the date will automatically change to today's date. This may not be what you intended. If you want the date to represent the date the file was created, then you could choose **Created on** from **Insert AutoText** on the Header and Footer toolbar (see Figure 2.4). You will come across fields again later.

Information: Page views

There are different ways of viewing a page. **Normal View** allows you to enter, edit and format text but does not show certain features of a page, for example the header and footer. Try this now – select **Normal** from the **View** menu. Notice how the page break appears as a dotted line across the document.

With **Print Layout View** you see the page as it will print with text and any graphics. This is called **WYSIWYG** **W**hat **Y**ou **S**ee **I**s **W**hat **Y**ou **G**et. Many people prefer working in this view. Select **Print Layout** from the **View** menu. Notice how the page ends and a new one begins, and how you can see the margins and any header and/or footer.

You can also change views using the buttons in the bottom left corner of the window (Figure 2.5).

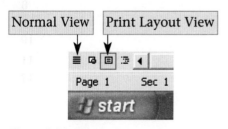

Figure 2.5 Page views

> **Information:** Page breaks
>
> A page break will naturally occur when the bottom of the page is reached. This is called a **soft page break** because it will alter automatically as text is added to, or deleted from, a document. A **hard page break** is one that is manually inserted and remains in position even when the document is edited.

Task 2.3	Insert and delete page breaks

Method

I	Using the same file (Working in Teams), position the cursor directly to the left of the subheading **Starting out**.
2	Select **Break** from the **Insert** menu.
3	Click on **Page break** and click **OK**.
4	Repeat in front of the subheading **The Team**.
5	Scroll through the document to see the effect.
6	To remove a page break, position the cursor directly to the left of the subheading **Starting out** and press **Backspace**.
7	Repeat in front of the subheading **The Team**.
8	Save the file.

> **Hint:**
>
> Shortcut – Hold down **Control** and press **Enter** to insert a page break (**Ctrl + Enter**).

Task 2.4	Edit a header or footer

To edit the header and footer, one way is to click on the **View** menu and select **Header and Footer** again. However, when in **Print Layout View**, you can double click on the header or footer text, which appears grey or dimmed, to edit it.

Method

I	Use the same file (Working in Teams).
2	Double click on the header itself for the header area to appear.
3	Delete your name and click on **Insert date**
4	Press the **Tab key** twice to move to the right margin.
5	Key in your name.
6	Switch to the footer and delete all the existing footer information.
7	Ensure the cursor is flashing at the left margin.
8	Click on **Insert AutoText**. Select **Filename**.
9	Press the **Tab key** twice to move to the right margin.
10	Click on **Insert AutoText** and select **Page X of Y**.
11	Close the Header and Footer toolbar Close
12	Save the file.

Information: Print preview

Checking your work is always important and **Print Preview** allows you to see how the document will print.

1 Click on the **Print Preview** button 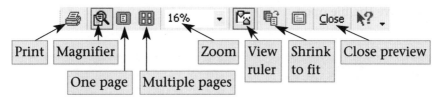 on the **Standard** toolbar. Preview opens (Figure 2.6). The mouse pointer changes to a magnifying glass when positioned over the selected page area. Click on the page to zoom in and click again to zoom out.

Figure 2.6 Print Preview toolbar

2 Click on the down arrow beside **Zoom** and select **50%**. Try other Zoom settings.
3 Click on the view **One Page** button.
4 Click on the **Magnifier** button. As the mouse pointer is moved over the text, it changes to an 'I beam'. Click on the page to edit. Click on again.
5 Click on the **Multiple Pages** button and drag across the first two 'pages' to view pages side by side (Figure 2.7).

This is very useful for checking the overall appearance of a document. You can see where the pages end, how the headers and footers look and when you have other objects, such as images or charts for example, you will have an impression of how effective and balanced the layout of the finished document will be.

6 **Shrink to Fit** (Figure 2.6) is useful for fitting a document onto one page if a few lines of text spill over onto a second page, by reducing the size of the text. Click on it now and notice the effect.

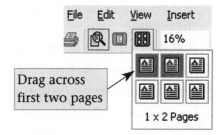

Drag across first two pages

Figure 2.7 View multiple pages

7 Click on the **Edit** menu and select **Undo** (Shrink to Fit) to undo the last action and revert back to two pages.
8 Click on **Close** on the Print Preview toolbar.
9 Save the file.

→ Practise your skills 2.1

1 Open a new file and key in the following text.

Conservatories today

Today's conservatories can make wonderful living spaces. Many people use them as an extra living room rather than a place to put their plants. If you are thinking about a conservatory there are a number of things you should consider.

What do you want to use it for?

Well, you think you want a conservatory but you must ask yourself what you really want to use it for. Is it for storing the plants over the winter? Is it somewhere just to while away summer evenings? Do you want to use it all the year round? Will it be a children's playroom? What furniture do you want to put in there? Is it big enough once the furniture is in there? How are you going to heat it? Do you need power and light? Is it likely to be an all-purpose room? →

2 Change the page setup to **A5** landscape with margins all round of **2 cm**.

3 Save the file as **Conservatory Use**.

4 Embolden the main heading and the subheading and change the font size to **14**.

5 Add your name in the centre of the header area.

6 Insert the filename in the left of the footer and the date on the right.

7 Proofread, print preview and spellcheck.

8 Save and print. Leave the file open.

→ Practise your skills 2.2

In this task you will open a new blank file and then copy and paste the text from two others files into it. You must then make sure the formatting is consistent.

1 Open the file **Conservatory** from **My Documents**.

2 Open a new blank document – you should now have three files open.

3 Key in the heading **So you want a conservatory?** and press **Enter** twice.

4 Save the file as **Buying a conservatory**.

5 Copy and paste the contents of the file **Conservatory** into this new file.

6 Copy and paste the contents of the file **Conservatory Use** to the end of this new file.

7 Insert a page break in front of the subheading **Conservatories today**.

8 Format all the text of the combined file as **Arial** size **12**, with **left alignment**.

9 Change the main heading to size **14** and bold.

10 Add your name in the header and the filename in the bottom left of the footer with the date on the right.

11 Adjust any spacing between paragraphs if necessary.

12 Delete the page break in front of the subheading **Conservatories today**.

13 Check, print preview, save and print.

→ Check your knowledge

1 Why are page numbers and page totals useful, e.g. Page 3 of 4?

2 What is a field?

3 State a limitation of using a field that inserts the date or time in a header or footer.

4 What is the importance of print preview?

5 What is the difference between hard and soft page breaks?

Organising your work

You will learn to

- Create folders as you save files
- Save files into folders
- Save files to floppy disk
- Create folders before saving

The number of files you work with grows very quickly, and just as you should organise your paper files, so you should do the same with your word processed files, so that you can find them easily later.

Information: Using folders

You should be aware from Level 1 of the importance of folders for organising your work and putting related files together. Folders should have a name that reflects the contents of the folder, as indeed should files themselves. Folders can be created as you save a file in Word. So far your files may have been saved straight into My Documents. If you have already created folders for Level 2, well done!

Remember:

Naming files with suitable names helps you to find them later.

Task 3.1 — Save a copy of a file and create a folder

Method

1   Use the same file **Working in Teams** from the previous task.
2   Click on **Save** 💾

This saves the file with the name it already has to the location you first saved it – probably My Documents. To save the file to a different location you must use **Save As**.

3   Select **Save As** from the **File** menu (Figure 3.1). Notice how the **Save in:** box currently reads **My Documents**.

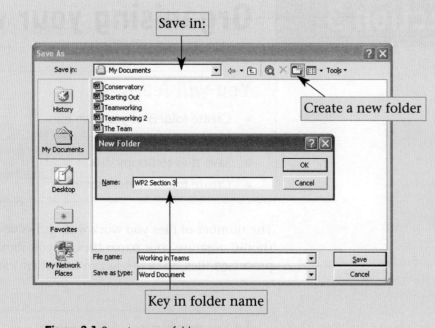

Figure 3.1 Save to a new folder

4   Click on **Create New Folder** 📁

5   Key in the folder name **WP2 Section 3** and click **OK**. Notice how the **Save in:** box now shows the new folder name, meaning the file will be saved into the new folder.

6   The original filename shows in the **Filename** box. Change this to **Copy of Working in Teams**.

7   Click on **Save**.

You now have a file called **Working in Teams** in **My Documents** and a copy of it in the folder **WP2 Section 3**. Using **Save As**, as you did above, allows you to save a copy of the file using a different name and to a different location. Copies are usually made of a file as a backup which means that should something happen to the original, then you still have the copy. You will now save a copy to floppy disk as well.

Task 3.2   Save to floppy disk

Method

1   Insert a floppy disk into the disk drive with the label uppermost and nearest to you (Figure 3.2). Push it gently, but firmly, into the drive.

2   Using the same file, select **Save As** from the **File** menu.

3   Click on the down arrow alongside the **Save in:** box (Figure 3.3). Notice how the computer has 'remembered' where you last saved – WP2 Section 3.

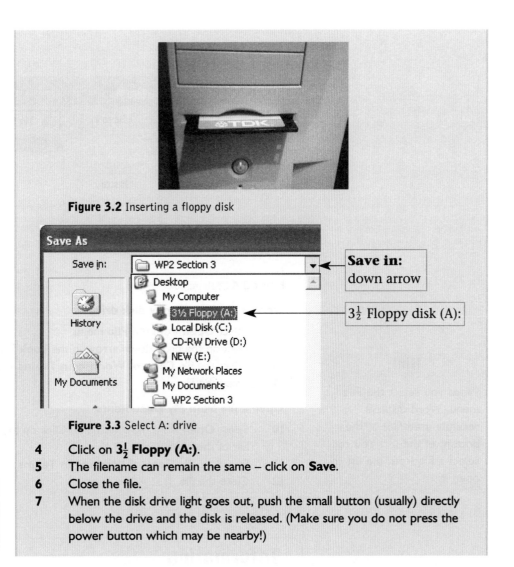

Figure 3.2 Inserting a floppy disk

Save in: down arrow

$3\frac{1}{2}$ Floppy disk (A):

Figure 3.3 Select A: drive

4   Click on **$3\frac{1}{2}$ Floppy (A:)**.
5   The filename can remain the same – click on **Save**.
6   Close the file.
7   When the disk drive light goes out, push the small button (usually) directly below the drive and the disk is released. (Make sure you do not press the power button which may be nearby!)

It would be a good idea at this point to make sure you can remember how to open files from folders. Ensure that all files are closed at this point.

Task 3.3 **Open files from different folders and locations**

Method

Open a file from a folder

1   Select **Open** from the **File** menu (Figure 3.4). Notice how the **Look in:** box has 'remembered' where you were last working – in this case on the floppy disk drive A:.
2   Click on **My Documents** in the left side bar of the open window.
3   Double click on the folder **WP2 Section 3**. The **Look in:** box should have changed accordingly.
4   Select the file **Copy of Working in Teams** and click on **Open**.
5   Close the file.

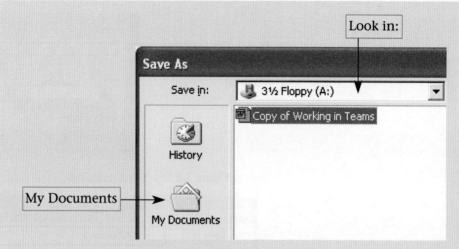

Figure 3.4 Look in: box

Open a file from floppy disk drive A:

6   Select **Open** from the **File** menu.
7   Click on the drop down arrow in the **Look in:** box and select **3½ floppy A:**.
8   Select the file **Copy of Working in Teams** and click on **Open**.
9   Close the file.

Open a file from My Documents

10   Select **Open** from the **File** menu. Click on **My Documents** in the left side bar of the open window.
11   Select the file **Copy of Working in Teams** and click on **Open**.
12   Close the file.

Hint:

When you select the File menu, Word displays recently used files at the bottom of the list. You can select a file from the list to open it.

Information

If you become 'lost' when saving and opening files, always click on **My Documents** in the left side bar of the Save/Open window and start from there!

Information: Create folders

Another way of creating folders is to do it in Windows itself, outside of Word.

Task 3.4   Create a folder before saving

Method

1   Click on **Minimize** in the top right-hand corner of the window to minimise the document window down to a button on the **taskbar** at the bottom of the screen (Figure 3.5).

Hint:

Clicking on the red **Close** button is another way of closing Word.

Note:

If My Documents is not visible, click on **Start →** **All Programs**. If it is still not visible, you may need to select **Windows Explorer** as it depends on your setup. Check with your tutor.

Hint:

To rename a folder, click the right mouse button on the folder name and choose **Rename**. Key in a new name.

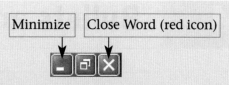

Figure 3.5 Minimize Word

2   Click on the **Start** menu and select **My Documents** (If this is not visible, see Note in margin.)

Figure 3.6 My Documents window

3   In the **My Documents** window (Figure 3.6) click on the **File** menu – **New** – **Folder**.

4   The new folder appears with the name highlighted – key in **WP2 Section 4** to replace the words **New Folder**.

5   Click on a blank area of the screen to deselect the folder name.

6   Return to Word by clicking on the Word button on the taskbar at the bottom of the screen.

→ Practise your skills 3.1

1   Open a new document and key in your name.

2   Save the file as **Name** into My Documents.

3   Save the file as **Name 2** onto floppy disk.

4   Save the file as **Name 3** into **WP2 Section 3** folder.

5   Save the file as **Name 4** into a new folder called **WP2 Skills Practice**.

6   Close the file.

7   Minimize Word and create a new folder in My Documents window called **Miscellaneous**.

→ Check your knowledge

1   What is C: drive?

2   What is the floppy disk drive also known as?

3   What is the purpose of a folder?

4   What must you wait for before removing a floppy disk?

5   What is a backup copy?

Section 4 — Bullets and numbering

You will learn to

- Create lists using bullet points
- Create numbered lists
- Use outline numbering

There are many ways of presenting text so that it is easier to read – breaking it into paragraphs is just one. Others are bullets and numbering, which are useful for clearly presenting items in a list.

Information: Bullets and numbering

Bullets are used to give emphasis to a list of items – as in the list of the topics at the beginning of each section of this book.

Numbering is used to automatically number a list of items.

Both can be applied before or after keying in a list.

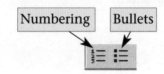

Figure 4.1 Numbering and bullets

Task 4.1 — Create lists using numbers and bullets

Method

1. Open a new file and key in **Planets of the Solar System**.
2. Press **Enter** twice and key in the following:
   The solar system consists of the Sun and nine planets that orbit around it. In order of distance from the Sun, these are:
3. Press **Enter** twice.
4. Click on the **Numbering** button (Figure 4.1) and key in **Mercury**. Notice how the button appears to be pressed in. (Numbers are indented from the margin.) Press **Enter**.
5. Key in the following, pressing **Enter** after each one.
   Venus
   Earth
   Mars
   Jupiter
   Saturn
   Uranus
   Neptune
   Pluto
6. Press **Enter** twice. Notice how the numbering stops.

Hint:

Numbered items can be moved back to the margin by clicking on **Decrease Indent** – see Task 4.2.

7 Highlight the list of planets excluding the heading and click on the **Numbering** button to remove them. The text moves back to the margin.

8 Highlight the list again and click on the **Bullets** button.

9 Highlight the list and click again on the **Bullets** button to remove them.

10 Spellcheck and proofread the document.

11 Add your name in the footer.

12 Save the document as **Solar System** into the **WP2 Section 4** folder.

Information: Secondary points

When working with lists you may sometimes have secondary points, for example:

- Here is an main point
  o This is a secondary point
  o This is a further secondary point
- This is another main point

Task 4.2	Create secondary points in a bulleted list

Method

1 Using the Solar System document created above, insert the line **Inner Solar System** before **Mercury**.

2 Insert the line **Outer Solar System** before **Jupiter**.

3 Highlight the entire list except the main heading and click on the **Bullets** button.

4 Highlight the first four planets – **Mercury**, **Venus**, **Earth** and **Mars** and click on the **Increase Indent** button (Figure 4.2).

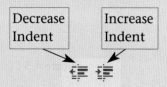

Figure 4.2 Decrease/Increase Indent buttons

5 Highlight the remaining five planets and click on **Increase Indent**.

Task 4.3	Change secondary items back to main items

Method

1 Highlight the first four planets and click on **Decrease Indent**.

2 Repeat for the remaining five planets. All items should now be main bullet points.

3 Save and close.

Information

The processes described in the last two tasks are often known as **promoting** and **demoting**. Promoting an item moves it to the left and makes it more ' important', whilst demoting moves it to the right and makes it less 'important'. The same method can be used for creating sub-items in a numbered list. Try this now with the same list. The secondary items will be numbered a, b, c, etc.

Information: Customise numbering

When numbering items you may want to customise numbering to start at a number other than number one.

Task 4.4   Customise numbering

Method

1   Close any files that may be open, start a new document and key in the following: **April, May, June, July, August**.

2   Highlight the list and click on the **Numbering** button.

3   With the list still highlighted, select **Bullets and Numbering** from the **Format** menu.

4   Click on **Customize** (Figure 4.3).

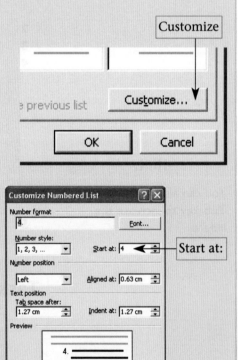

Figure 4.3 Customise numbering

Figure 4.4 Start numbering

5   Click in the **Start at:** box (Figure 4.4), key in **4** and click **OK**.

Notice how you can also change the number format and the indent if desired (Figure 4.4).

> ## Information: Customise bullets
>
> Sometimes you may want to change the style of the bullets, for example to create tick boxes for a checklist.

Task 4.5   Change bullet style

Method

1   Using the same document as above, highlight the list and click on the **Bullets** button.
2   Select **Bullets and Numbering** from the **Format** menu.
3   Click on the **Tick box** style (Figure 4.5) and click **OK**.
4   Save as **Tick boxes** into the folder **WP2 Section 4**, print and close.

Hint:

If you do not see the tick box style, click on **Customize** and then **Character**.

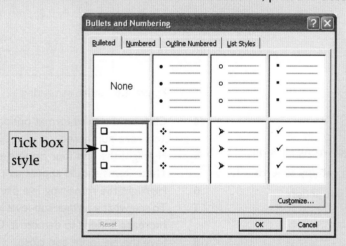

Figure 4.5 Change bullet style

> ## Information: Outline numbering
>
> Some documents may require more complex numbering, particularly formal documents. **Outline numbering** allows up to nine levels of numbering, for example
>
> 1   First main point
>   1.1. Secondary item
>   1.1.1. sub-item
>   1.1.2. another sub-item
>   1.2. Secondary item
> 2   Second main point
>   2.1. Secondary item
>   2.2. Secondary item
>   2.2.1. sub-item

Task 4.6 — Use outline numbering

Method

1. Open the file **Solar System** from the **WP2 Section 4** folder. First remove any bullets or numbers remaining.
2. With all items highlighted, select the **Format** menu and **Bullets and Numbering**.
3. Select the **Outline Numbered** tab (Figure 4.6).

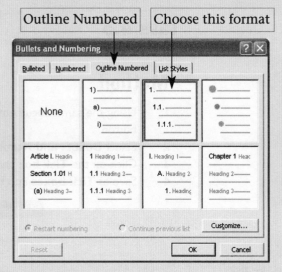

Outline Numbered   Choose this format

Figure 4.6 Outline numbering

Remember:

If things go wrong click on **Undo** ↻ at any time to undo the last action.

4. Click on the third format option of the four on the top row and click **OK**. All items are numbered.
5. Highlight the first four planets and click on **Increase Indent** to demote them. These items should appear as 1.1, 1.2, etc.
6. Highlight the remaining five planets and click on **Increase Indent**.
7. To see what a further sub-level looks like, click on one of the planets and click on **Increase Indent** to demote it. Click on **Decrease Indent** to promote it again.
8. Save the file, print and close.

Information: Creating outline numbered lists as text is keyed in

In the task above you have created outline lists after keying in the text. Sometimes you will want to do this as you key in the text.

Task 4.7 — Create an outline list as text is keyed in

Method

1. Open a new document, key in **Holiday Destinations** and press **Enter** twice.
2. Click on the **Numbering** button, key in **Canary Islands** and press **Enter** once.

Hint:

You can also press the

Tab key to

increase the indent.

Remember:

Always check unusual words or proper names against the original text.

Hint:

Shift + Enter starts a new line but not a new paragraph so the numbering continues.

3   Click on the **Increase Indent** button and key in **Tenerife**.
4   Select **Bullets and Numbering** from the **Format** menu and click on the **Outline Numbered** tab (Figure 4.6).
5   Choose the third option out of the three on the top row and click **OK**. Notice how the style changes from **a** to **1.1** and also how the main item Canary Islands is no longer indented from the margin.
6   Press **Enter** and key in **La Gomera**.
7   Press **Enter** and key in **Gran Canaria**.
8   Press **Enter** and key in **Fuerteventura**.
9   Press **Enter** and key in **Lanzarote**.
10 Press **Enter**. As the outline list is now complete, click on **Decrease Indent**.
11 Key in **Morocco** and press **Enter**.
12 Click on **Increase Indent** and key in **Agadir**.
13 Press **Enter** and key in **Marrakesh**.
14 Press **Enter** and click on **Decrease Indent**.
15 Key in **Malta** and press **Enter**.
16 Click on **Increase Indent** and key in **Valletta**.
17 Press **Enter** and key in **Sliema**.
18 Press **Enter** and key in **Gozo**.
19 Press **Enter** twice to finish the list.
20 Save as **Holiday Destinations** into the **WP2 Section 4** folder.
21 Proofread the spelling of the place names carefully against the original, correct and resave if necessary.
22 Print and close.

Information: Outline numbered lists and paragraph spacing

If you require a space between paragraphs you normally press Enter twice. In the case of numbering (or bullets), this would cancel numbering and end the list. One solution is to press **Shift + Enter** to leave a blank line (hold Shift key down and press Enter), and then **Enter** for a new line and to continue numbering.

Task 4.8	Create an outline list with spacing between lines

Method

1   Start a new file.
2   Using your printout of **Holiday destinations**, recreate the document with a space between each item in the list – each time you start a new item press **Shift + Enter** and then **Enter**, remembering to decrease/increase indent where necessary.
3   Check your work, save as **Holidays** into the **WP2 Section 4** folder and print.

Information

Sometimes you may key in all the text first without numbering and then highlight it and add the numbering afterwards.

Information: Agenda and minutes

An agenda is a list of items to be discussed at a meeting, also showing the time, date and place that the meeting is to be held. Minutes are a record of what was discussed at a meeting. A short agenda might be printed on A5, although A4 is a general-purpose size and used for most documents. Minutes would be printed on A4.

→ Practise your skills 4.1

1 Open a new file and key in the heading **Avalon Sports and Social Club**, **bold**, size **16**.

2 Press **Enter** and key in **Meeting to be held on 9ᵗʰ January 2004 at 12.30 pm in the Board Room**. Embolden this line and change the text size to **12**.

3 Change the page setup to **A5 landscape** with left and right margins of **3.5 cm**.

4 Press **Enter** twice and key in **Agenda**. Embolden.

5 Press **Enter** twice, and create the following bulleted list:

   Minutes of the last meeting
   Treasurer's Report
   Quiz Evening
   Summer River Trip
   Any Other Business

6 Change the bullets to numbering.

7 Key in the following as a separate paragraph at the bottom of the page:

   Following the meeting at approximately 1 pm, there will be a buffet lunch to mark the retirement of Bob Dawson and to thank him for all his hard work over the last few years as our Treasurer.

8 Spellcheck, proofread your work and print preview.

9 Insert a footer with the filename on the left and your name on the right. (The filename will display as Document1 until the file is saved.)

10 Save as **Agenda** into the **WP2 Skills Practice** folder.

11 Print and close.

→ Practise your skills 4.2

1 Open a new A4 document and create the following:

   Avalon Sports and Social Club
   Minutes of the meeting held on 9 January 2004
   Present:

Kevin Bailey	**Chi Wai Lee**
Bob Dawson	**Peter Marshall**
Emma Hart	**Dan Watson**
Ursula Johannsen	

Create a numbered list, using the **Outline Numbered** option.

For each sub-item use the **Increase Indent** button.

1. **Minutes of the last meeting – the minutes were agreed.**

2. **Treasurer's Report**
   2.1. **Dan has taken over the role of Treasurer and reported that there was £356 in the account.**
   2.2. **The new signatories had now been set up.**

3. **Quiz Evening**
   3.1. **Kevin agreed to produce the questions.**
   3.2. **It was agreed that two bottles of wine would be provided for each team and crisps and nuts would be placed on each table.**
   3.3. **Ursula volunteered to buy the raffle prizes.**

4. **Summer River Trip**
   4.1. **The response from staff was good. It was therefore agreed to book this now with a limit of 50 people.**
   4.2. **Chi Wai volunteered to produce posters and to advertise the event in the newsletter requesting a deposit of £5 per person straight away.**

5. **Any Other Business**
   5.1. **Bob Dawson's farewell buffet went off very well.**
   5.2. **All committee members will try to encourage other members of staff to join.**
   5.3. **The next meeting was arranged for February 13th.**

2 Embolden the first two lines and each main item, i.e. 1, 2, 3, 4 and 5.

3 Format the first two lines to size **16**.

4 Change the font throughout to **Arial**.

5 Proofread, print preview and spellcheck.

6 Create a header with the filename on the left and your name on the right.

7 Save as **Minutes** into the **WP2 Skills Practice** folder. Print and close.

→ **Check your knowledge**

1 What is the purpose of bullets and numbering?

2 What is outline numbering?

3 What is an agenda?

4 What are minutes?

5 What would you do to demote an item in a list?

Consolidation 1

1. Create a folder called **Consolidation**.

2. Open a new A4 document with margins all round of 3 cm and create the following:

Warren First School Activity Day

We are pleased to give you more information about the Activity Day. There are four activities to choose from and we hope the children will enjoy the coaching sessions.

Choose two out of the four activities listed by ticking the boxes below.

- ☐ **Badminton**
- ☐ **Football**
- ☐ **Tennis**
- ☐ **Swimming**

Create a bulleted list and change the style to tick boxes

The following items will be required for each activity:

1. **Badminton**
   1.1. **Shorts and T Shirt**
   1.2. **Trainers**

2. **Football**
   2.1. **Shorts and T Shirt**
   2.2. **Football boots**

3. **Swimming**
   3.1. **Swimming Trunks/Costume**
   3.2. **Towel**
   3.3. **Plastic bag for wet gear**

4. **Tennis**
   4.1. **Shorts and T Shirt**
   4.2. **Trainers**

Create a numbered list and use the **Outline Numbered** option.

For each sub-item use the **Increase Indent** button.

Press Shift + Enter and then Enter between each main item, or if you forget and numbering stops, click on the Numbering button to restart it.

All children will require a packed lunch and plenty of drinks especially if the weather should be particularly warm. Normal start and finish times apply – please make sure the children arrive promptly in the morning.

Please return the slip below to your child's class teacher.

Child's name

3. Embolden the main heading and format to size **16**.

4. Cut the paragraph beginning **Choose two out of the four . . .** and the tick box list, and paste it below the last line **Child's name**. Adjust the spacing if necessary.

5. After the line starting **Please return the slip below . . .** press **Enter** three times and key in a dotted line using the full stop.

6. In the first paragraph after the first sentence, insert **Each child will take part in two activities**.

7. Create a header with your name and a footer that displays the date on the left and the page number on the right, starting at page 3 as it will be used to form part of a longer document.

8. Proofread, print preview and spellcheck.

9. Save the document as **Activity Day** into the **Consolidation** folder and print.

10. Save a copy of the document onto floppy disk and close.

Section 5 | Paragraph formatting

You will learn to

- Indent paragraphs
- Change line spacing
- Add borders and shading

Paragraphs are used to divide a page where a natural change in thought or topic occurs. This makes it much easier to read than continuous text and also improves the appearance of a document. There are a number of ways that particular paragraphs might be formatted to make them stand out, such as giving them headings or subheadings, indenting, adding a border or shading.

Information: Indented paragraphs

Using the **Increase Indent** button can also be used to indent whole paragraphs of text from the left margin. This makes a paragraph stand out from the remainder of the text. It is also possible to indent from both the left and the right margin. Indenting affects complete paragraphs, so to indent one paragraph, the cursor has only to be positioned within that paragraph. To indent two or more consecutive paragraphs, you must highlight them first.

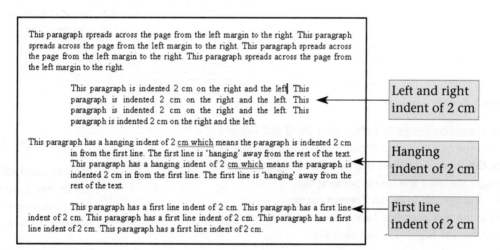

Figure 5.1 Indented paragraphs

Task 5.1 | Indent a paragraph from the left

Method

I	Open the file **Starting Out** in **My documents**.
2	Position the cursor in the last paragraph and click on the **Increase Indent** button – the paragraph moves to the right.
3	Click on **Increase Indent** again – the paragraph moves further to the right.
4	Click on **Decrease Indent** twice, to take the text back to its original position.

Using **Increase Indent**, indent by one tab stop (1.27 cm) each time you press it. The following method allows you to specify the position of the indent.

Method

1   Using the same file **Starting Out**, click in the last paragraph.
2   Select **Paragraph** from the **Format** menu (Figure 5.2).

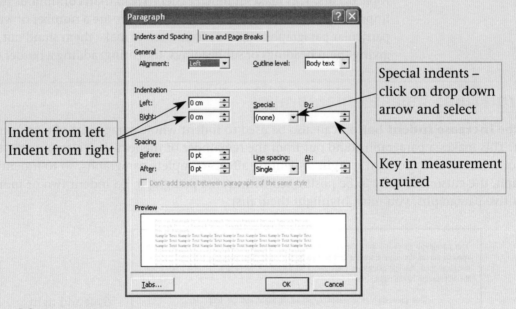

Indent from left
Indent from right

Special indents – click on drop down arrow and select

Key in measurement required

Figure 5.2 Indent paragraph

3   Click in the box alongside **Left**, delete the **0** and key in **I**.
4   Click in the box alongside **Right**, delete the **0** and key in **I**.
5   Click **OK**. Note how the paragraph has changed.
6   Highlight the third and fourth paragraphs.
7   Select **Paragraph** from the **Format** menu.
8   Click in the box alongside **Left**, delete the **0** and key in **2**.
9   Repeat for the **Right** side and click **OK**.

Hint:

You can also click on the up or down arrow beside the measurement to change the indent.

Hint:

If indenting goes 'wrong', highlight all affected paragraphs and set the indent on both sides to 0 using **Paragraph** from the **Format** menu.

Method

1   Highlight the last three paragraphs.
2   Select **Paragraph** from the **Format** menu.
3   Click in the box alongside **Left** and key in **0**.
4   Repeat for the **Right** side and click **OK**.

Information: Indenting paragraphs using the ruler

It is also possible to change paragraph indents using the horizontal ruler at the top of the window below the toolbars. If the horizontal ruler is not displayed, select **Ruler** from the **View** menu. (A tick next to the ruler indicates the ruler is displayed.)

In Figure 5.3 the indent markers are displayed on the left and right margins on the ruler. To indent, position the cursor in a paragraph or highlight several paragraphs, and drag the left indent marker and/or the right indent marker to the required position. Dragging the left indent marker (the small rectangle) causes the two markers above it to move at the same time. (The first line indent marker changes the first line of a paragraph only, and the hanging indent marker affects the rest of a paragraph.)

Figure 5.3 Indent using the ruler

Remember:

Drag means to hold the left mouse button down and move the mouse in the required direction.

Remember:

Dragging the left indent marker causes the two markers above it to move at the same time.

Task 5.4 — Indent a paragraph using the ruler

Method

1   Position the cursor in the last paragraph.
2   Drag the **left indent marker** (the small rectangle) to the **1 cm** point on the ruler (Figure 5.3).
3   Drag the **right indent marker** to the **14 cm** point on the ruler.
4   Highlight the third and fourth paragraphs and drag the **left indent marker** to the **2 cm** point on the ruler.
5   Repeat for the right side.

Task 5.5 — Remove indent using the ruler

Remember:

If indenting goes 'wrong', highlight all affected paragraphs and set the indent on both sides to 0 using **Paragraph** from the **Format** menu.

Method

1   Highlight the last three paragraphs.
2   Drag the left indent marker back to the left margin (0).
3   Drag the right indent marker back to the right margin.
4   Make sure no paragraphs are still indented. Close the file *without saving*.

Information: Line spacing

Line spacing is the amount of space between one line of text and another. Single spacing is the default. Double spacing is often used for draft copies of documents to give space for amendments to be made by hand before the final copy is produced. Spacing is changed by either positioning the cursor inside a paragraph, highlighting several paragraphs together or even the entire document (**Edit** menu – **Select All**) and then applying the new line spacing.

Task 5.6 Change line spacing

Method

1 Open the file **Starting Out** from **My documents** and position the cursor in the *last* paragraph.

2 Select **Paragraph** from the **Format** menu (Figure 5.4). Ensure the **Indents and Spacing** tab is selected.

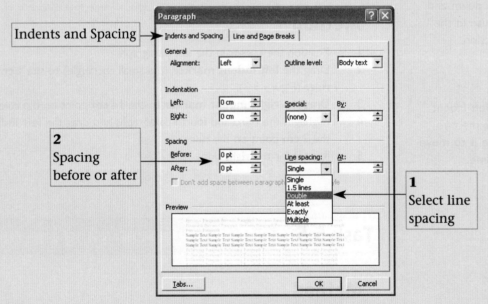

Figure 5.4 Spacing

3 Click on the drop down arrow under **Line spacing** (labelled I in Figure 5.4) and select **Double**. Click **OK**.

4 Highlight all paragraphs and repeat this procedure selecting **I.5 lines**.

Now experiment with the keyboard shortcuts for line spacing shown below, ending up with the document in single line spacing.

Single	**Control + 1**	the default setting
Double	**Control + 2**	leaves one clear line space between lines, often used for draft documents
1.5	**Control + 5**	leaves one-and-a-half line space between lines

Line spacing commands only affect the paragraph in which the cursor is placed unless you highlight several paragraphs or the entire document.

Information: Spacing before and after a paragraph

The spacing before and after a paragraph can be varied without affecting the paragraph itself.

Task 5.7 | **Change spacing before and after paragraphs**

Using the same file as above – **Starting Out** – ensure all line spacing is set on Single before starting.

Method

1   Highlight all text and select **Paragraph** from the **Format** menu.
2   In the **Spacing** section (labelled 2 in Figure 5.4), click on the up arrow alongside **After** to change the spacing to **12 pt**. This equates to one normal line space.
3   Click **OK**.
4   Repeat this procedure changing the spacing **Before** and **After** to **6 pt**. Click **OK**.
5   Change it back to **0**.

Information: Borders and shading

Borders can be applied to single or to several paragraphs, to make them stand out effectively. Shading (greys or colour) can also be used in conjunction with borders or used alone.

Task 5.8 | **Apply borders and shading**

Method

Use the same file as above.

1   Click into the last paragraph and select **Borders and Shading** from the **Format** menu. Ensure the **Borders** tab is selected (Figure 5.5).

2   Select a line style from the list (scroll through the styles).

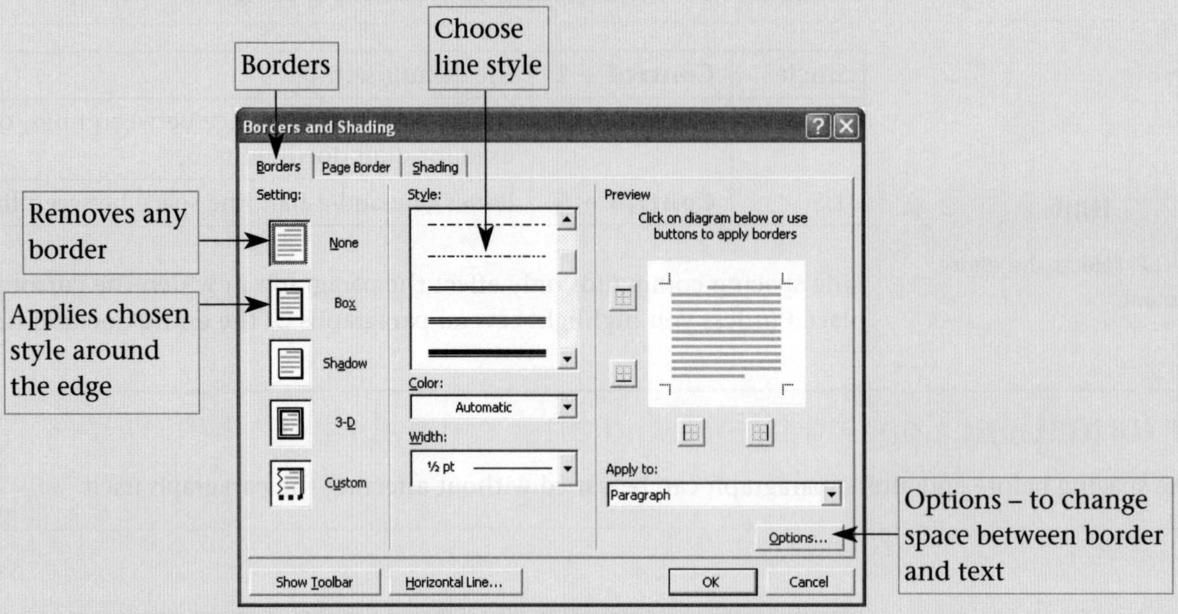

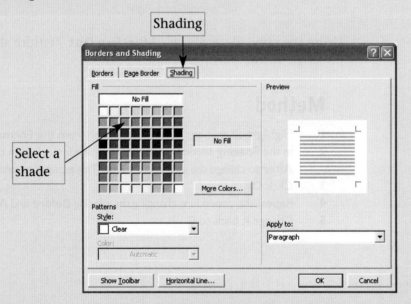

Figure 5.5 Borders

3   Click on **Box** setting.

Figure 5.6 Apply shading

4   Click on the **Shading** tab (Figure 5.6) and select a pale grey shade.
5   Click **OK**.

Try out different combinations of borders and shading on this file, and then close it without saving.

→ Practise your skills 5.1

1 Open an **A4** document with default margins.
2 Key in the heading **Paragraphs** and format it as size **16, bold**.
3 Key in the text shown in Figure 5.1 as four straightforward paragraphs.
4 Justify the text.
5 Indent the second paragraph by **2 cm** on each side.
6 Create a hanging indent of **2 cm** for the third paragraph.
7 Create a first line indent of **2 cm** for the last paragraph.
8 Add your name and the filename in the footer.
9 Save as **Paragraphs** into the **WP2 Skills Practice** folder.
10 Add a simple border to the first paragraph.
11 Apply pale grey shading to the second paragraph.
12 Apply a broken line style border and a different grey shading to the third paragraph.
13 Apply a double line style border to the last paragraph.
14 Change the line spacing of the first paragraph to **double**.
15 Change the line spacing of the second paragraph to **1.5**.
16 Highlight all paragraphs and apply a space of **12 pt** after each paragraph.
17 Proofread, spellcheck and print preview.
18 Save as **Paragraphs with borders** and print.

→ Practise your skills 5.2

1 Open the file **Buying a Conservatory** from My Documents.
2 Add a border and light grey shading to the second paragraph.
3 Change the line spacing of this paragraph to **1.5** and indent by **1 cm** on each side.
4 Save the file as **Buying a Conservatory 2** into the **WP2 Skills Practice** folder.

→ Check your knowledge

1 What is the purpose of paragraphs?
2 What is the keyboard shortcut for double line spacing?
3 What is the keyboard shortcut for 1.5 line spacing?
4 What is the purpose of using borders and shading?
5 Shading can be applied without a border. True or False?
6 Identify the three markers shown in Figure 5.7.

Figure 5.7

Checking and proofreading

You will learn to

- Use the spellcheck and add words to the dictionary
- Understand the importance of proofreading and accuracy

In business, the accuracy of documents is vital. The spellcheck will help in this respect but there is no substitute for careful visual checking of your work.

Information: Checking spelling

You should automatically be using the spellcheck by now to check your work. There will always be words that the spellcheck does not recognise, such as proper names, although you may use them frequently. These words appear with a red wavy line below but it does not necessarily mean they are wrong. Any words you are likely to use again should be added to the dictionary.

Task 6.1 | Check spelling and add to the dictionary

Method

1   Open a new document and key in:

Framley was a picturesque village coming runner-up in the Best-kept Village Competition. Bettington came first.

2   Press **Enter** and key in your name and your own home town.

3   Click on the **Spelling and Grammar** check button

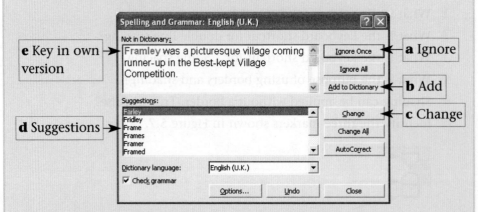

Figure 6.1 Spelling and Grammar

The spellcheck will stop at the first word **Framley** as it does not recognise it and you have the following choices (Figure 6.1):

a **Ignore** – if you are satisfied the word is correct.

b **Add** – if you know you will need this word in future and you want to add it to the dictionary.

c **Change** – to accept the highlighted suggested spelling.

d **Suggestions** – click on one of the listed suggested words and then click on **Change**.

e Key in your own version of the word and then click on **Change**.

4 Click on **Add**. Continue, adding Bettington and your own name and town.

Hint:

To spellcheck only part of a document, highlight that section first.

Green wavy lines under words relate to possible errors in grammar. If you do not want to check grammar, click in the check box **Check Grammar** in the bottom left corner of the Spelling and Grammar dialogue box to remove the tick.

Information: Proofreading

The spellcheck is a useful tool but there is no substitute for careful proofreading. Proofreading is not just about reading your work through but checking it – see the list below. It concerns not only the content but also the layout of a document as well, including any graphics. Proofreading was fully covered in Level 1 but it is an extremely important topic that is re-visited here.

Very often in business the only communication an organisation has with its clients or customers is by letters or other documents, such as reports or advertisements. Any impression that might be formed may be given only by the documents, and therefore they stand to represent that organisation. It is no different when creating documents for yourself. If, for example, you are applying for a job, you naturally want to give the best impression you can.

When working from original documents it is obviously vital that you copy carefully. You must copy names accurately to avoid offending or annoying the recipient, or at the very least, appearing careless. Ensure you reproduce any numbers correctly. A mistyped number could mean a wrong quantity is supplied and cost you or your organisation a fortune! A wrong telephone number could lose that all-important call. A wrong date could mean a lost meeting. A wrong amount of money could lose a contract. An error might cause a problem on a legal technicality so the consequences of that typing error might be huge! Does the document convey the intended meaning?

You should always:

- Check onscreen for misuse of words that the spellcheck has not picked up.
- Ensure the document conveys the meaning that was intended.
- Check carefully against the original text you may be working from.
- Check the correct forms of words have been used, e.g. their/there, border/boarder, where/were.
- Make sure that British English spellings are used and not American English.
- Check spelling of names, foreign words and any specialist/technical words.
- Check numbers to make sure they are correct and valid.
- Check any dates to make sure they are correct and valid, e.g. is it the right date, does the correct day match with the date?
- Check the layout carefully. Is everything lined up properly, are images in the right position, is the text readable around graphics?
- Check for consistency in fonts and sizes. Do they change in the middle of a document?
- Check graphics. Are they in the right place, is the text readable around them?
- Check after making any amendments.
- Print preview the page. Does it look right?
- Check the document again after printing.
- Check with the originator of the document if applicable.

➜ Practise your skills 6.1

1 Key in the following text, making the corrections by inserting or deleting text where indicated.

2 Add your name in the header with the date and filename in the footer.

3 Save as **Skills Practice 6** into the **WP2 Skills Practice** folder and print.

4 Spellcheck and proofread your printout carefully against the original to make sure you have made the amendments as shown.

OUTPUT DEVICES

(Visual Display Units)

VDUs are available in different sizes measured diagonally across the screen. The screen image is made up of little squares called pixels. The number of pixels affects the clarity of the image and the more pixels, the higher the resolution. ~~A higher resolution is desirable~~.

Another name for a VDU is a monitor.

Printers – The most common type of printers are the **laser printer** and the **ink-jet**. ~~Another type of printer is the dot matrix but these are not often used nowadays.~~

The **laser printer** uses a laser beam to build up an image in much the same way as a photocopier and produces a very clear, crisp output. They are more expensive than ink-jets although they have come down ~~quite~~ considerably in price ~~and colour laser printers are extremely expensive~~.

The **ink-jet printer** sprays minute drops of ink onto the ~~printer~~ paper. Images are built up from dots. They can give high quality output but need good quality paper.

These are measured as dots per inch or dpi.

➜ Practise your skills 6.2

1 Using the same document as above, key in the following sentences:
   A All staff will receive a pay increase of 2.75% with effect from the 12th of February.
   B The A487 leads from Fishguard to Cardigan via Eglwyswrw.
   C Sven-Goran Erikkson leads the England football team.
   D Steven Spielberg was born on 18 December 1946 in Cincinnati, Ohio.
   E Ingredients for Yorkshire pudding are 75 g of plain flour, 1 egg, 75 ml of milk, 50 ml of water plus salt and pepper.

2 Save the document and print.

3 Check your printout carefully against the original, taking particular care to check all figures and spellings of proper names.

4 Amend and resave if necessary.

➜ Check your knowledge

1 What is the purpose of adding new words to the dictionary?

2 What are the limitations of spellcheckers?

3 List as many things as you can that you should check when proofreading.

4 Why is it important to check your document for accuracy, correctness and meaning?

5 When proofreading, what else should you check apart from content.

Section 7 Tabs

You will learn to

- Create tables using different types of tab alignment
- Change tab types
- Use leader tabs

Tabulation is the arrangement of text and numbers in columns making the text easier to read and to stand out from other text. This can be achieved either by using **tabs** or Word's **Table** feature. This section covers the use of tabs.

Information: Tabulation

Tab stops can be set across the page at points where you wish to line up text. There are several different types of tab that affect the way this happens. The most commonly used are:

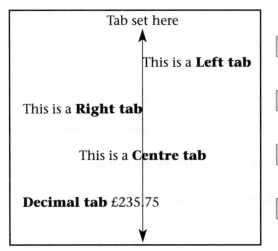

L Left tab aligns **left** at the tab setting

J Right tab aligns **right** at the tab setting

⊥ Centre tab aligns **centre** at the tab setting

⅃ Decimal tab aligns **decimal points** at the tab setting

By default, left tabs are set every 1.27 cm ($\frac{1}{2}$ inch) across the page. You can see these as light grey marks just below the ruler. (If the ruler is not displayed, select **Ruler** from the **View** menu.) When a new tab is set, the default tabs to the left of it are cleared. To set a tab, you click on the Tab button (Figure 7.1) to select the type of tab required (it changes each time you click on it), and then click on the horizontal ruler at the point where the tab is required. A tab marker appears.

Click Tab button to change tab type

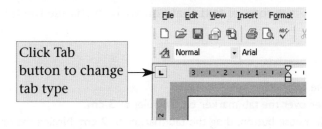

Figure 7.1 Tab button

Task 7.1   Setting tabs using the ruler

Method

1. Open a new document, key in the heading **Book Stock Codes** and press **Enter** twice.
2. Check left tab $\boxed{\text{L}}$ is selected on the Tab button and click on the ruler at **3 cm** to set a tab. Notice a left tab marker appears on the ruler (Figure 7.2).

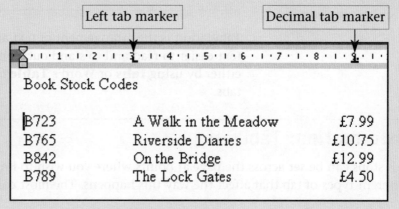

Figure 7.2 Setting tabs

3. Click on the **Tab** button three times until the decimal tab $\boxed{\text{⊥}}$ displays and click on the ruler at **9 cm**. Notice how a decimal tab marker appears.
4. Key in **B723** and press the **Tab** key.
5. Key in **A Walk in the Meadow** and press **Tab** key.
6. Key in **£7.99** and press **Enter** for a new line.
7. Repeat for the next three lines pressing **Tab** to move across the page and **Enter** to start a new line.
8. Save the file as **Books** into a new folder in **My documents** naming the folder **WP2 Section 7**.
9. Spellcheck and proofread. Resave if necessary.
10. Print.

Hint:

The Tab key is on the left of the keyboard above Caps Lock.

Task 7.2   Change tab settings

Before you change a tab that you have already set, you must highlight all the rows of text that you wish to change the tab settings for.

Method

1. Highlight all lines *of the table only*.
2. Position mouse pointer over the tab marker on the ruler at **3 cm**.
3. Holding down the left mouse button, drag the tab marker to **2 cm**. Notice the vertical line that appears to assist (Figure 7.3).

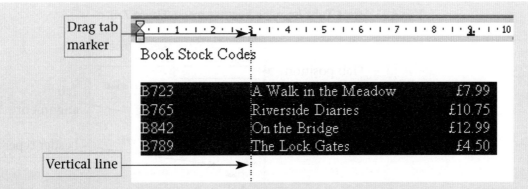

Figure 7.3 Change tab settings

4 Drag the tab marker set at **9 cm** to **8 cm**.
5 Click off the highlighted text to cancel highlighting.
6 Save the file as **Books 2** into **WP2 Section 7** folder.
7 Print and close.

Hint:

Click **Undo** ↶ if this goes wrong and try again.

> ### Information: Remove a tab
>
> To remove a tab, highlight the text from which the tab is to be removed, click on the tab marker in the ruler and drag downwards. It disappears.

> ### Information: Setting tabs using the Format menu
>
> Tabs can also be set by selecting **Tabs** from the **Format** menu to specify tab positions and tab type using precise measurements.

Task 7.3	**Set tabs using the Format menu**

Method

1 Open a new document and change the page setup to **A5 landscape** with margins of **2.5 cm** all round.
2 Key in the following:
Leisure sports
3 Press **Enter** twice.

4 Select **Tabs** from the **Format** menu (Figure 7.4).

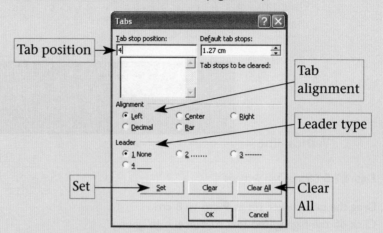

Figure 7.4 Setting tabs

5 In the **Tab stop position** box, key in **4** and click on **Set**. Notice the alignment is set on **Left**.
6 In the **Tab stop position** box, key in **8** and click on **Set**. Notice the alignment is set on **Left**. Click **OK**.
7 Key in **Tennis** and press the **Tab** key.
8 Key in **Squash** and press the **Tab** key.
9 Key in **Swimming** and press **Enter** to start a new line.
10 Complete the following pressing **Tab** between each item and **Enter** at the end of the line:

Football	**Badminton**	**Rugby**
Aerobics	**Running**	**Bowls**
Hockey	**Cycling**	**Fencing**

11 Save the document as **Sports** into the **WP2 Section 7** folder.

Task 7.4   Change tab settings using the Format menu

This task will use centre and right alignment tabs.

Method

1 Highlight all lines *of the table only*.
2 Select **Tabs** from the **Format** menu (Figure 7.4).
3 Click on **Clear All** to clear the existing tab settings.
4 In the **Tab stop position** box, key in **5** and click on **Center** alignment. Click on **Set**.
5 In the **Tab stop position** box, key in **11** and click on **Right** alignment. Click on **Set**.
6 Click **OK** and save.

Notice how the middle column is centred at the tab position and the last column is aligned to the right of the tab marker, each line ending at the tab.

Information: Leader tabs

A dotted, broken or solid line can be used to draw (or lead) the eye across the page making it easier to read a table. These are often known as **leader dots** and can be used for layouts such as contents pages or price lists, for example

Section 2 .... Page 3

Section 3 .... Page 7

Apart from dotted lines, other leader tab styles are broken lines and a continous line, for example

Section 4 _ Page 9

Section 4 _____ Page 9

Task 7.5   Set leader tabs

This task will use leader tabs with decimal alignment.

Method

Use the same file as above – **Sports** – leaving a space below the table.

1   Key in **Price per hour** at the left margin and press **Enter** twice.
2   Select **Tabs** from the **Format** menu (Figure 7.4).
3   Click on **Clear All** to clear the existing tab settings.
4   In the **Tab stop position** box, key in **9** and click on **Decimal** alignment.
5   Click on leader tab style 2.
6   Click on **Set**. Click **OK**.
7   Key in **Tennis**, press the **spacebar** to leave one space and then press the **Tab** key.
8   Key in **£5.75** and press **Enter**.
9   Key in **Squash**, press the **spacebar**, press the **Tab** key.
10   Key in **£7.50** and press **Enter**.
11   Key in **Swimming**, press the **spacebar**, press the **Tab** key.
12   Key in **£2.50** and press **Enter**.
13   Save the file, print and close.

Hint:

It is usual to leave one space before the start of the leader dots.

→ Practise your skills 7.1

Create this table setting tabs *using the ruler.*

1 Open a new **A5 landscape** page with margins of **3 cm** all round.
2 Key in the heading **Evening Courses** and press **Enter** twice.
3 Set a **centre tab** at **6.5 cm** and **left tabs** at **9** and **12 cm**.
4 Key in the column headings below and press **Enter** twice.
5 Key in the remaining data.

Subject	Weeks	Day	Time
Word Processing Level 1	20	Monday	18.30
Presentation Graphics	10	Tuesday	18.00
Spreadsheets	36	Tuesday	18.30
Word Processing Level 2	20	Wednesday	19.00
Spreadsheets Introduction	10	Wednesday	19.00
Desktop Publishing Level 1	20	Thursday	18.00
Databases	22	Thursday	19.00

6 Embolden the main heading and enlarge to size **16**.
7 Embolden the column headings and enlarge to size **14**.
8 Proofread carefully, particularly the figures, spellcheck and print preview.
9 Save as **Evening Courses** into the **WP2 Skills Practice** folder, print and close.

→ Practise your skills 7.2

Create this table setting tabs *using Tabs from the Format menu.*

1 Open a new **A5 landscape** document with top and bottom margins of **3.5 cm** and left and right margins of **4 cm**.
2 Key in the heading and the first paragraph below.
3 Set **centre tabs** at **6** and **10 cm**.
4 Key in the column headings and press **Enter** twice.
5 Remove the tabs and replace with **decimal tabs** at **7** and **10 cm**.
6 Key in the remaining data.

Course Fees

A list of course fees is given below. If there are any queries concerning these, please refer to Paul Adams, Client Centre Manager, on Extension 7321.

Duration	Fees	Exam Fee
10 week courses	£25.00	£4.50
20 week courses	£50.00	£7.00
22 week courses	£55.00	£7.00
36 week courses	£75.00	£12.50

7 Embolden and enlarge the main heading to size **17**.
8 Embolden and enlarge the column headings to size **14**.
9 Enlarge the remaining text to size **14**.
10 Proofread carefully, spellcheck and print preview.
11 Save as **Course Fees** into the **WP2 Skills Practice** folder, print and close.

→ Practise your skills 7.3

Create this table *using Tabs from the Format menu*.

1 Open a new **A5 landscape** page using default margins.

2 Set a **left tab** at **2 cm** and a **decimal leader tab** at **13 cm**.

3 Key in the data below.

College Canteen

The canteen is open in the evenings between 5.30 and 6.45 pm as a service to those students arriving for their evening class straight from work.

Toasted sandwich £1.75
Bacon roll £1.50
Soup and roll £1.90
Vegetable pasta £2.60
Jacket potato and salad £2.10

Tea, coffee and cold drinks are available from the vending machines.

Crisps and chocolate also available from vending machines.

4 Embolden the main heading and change to size **18**.

5 Enlarge the remaining text to size **14**.

6 Centre all text except the price list.

7 Proofread carefully, spellcheck and print preview.

8 Save as **College Canteen** into the **WP2 Skills Practice** folder, print and close.

→ Check your knowledge

1 Identify the following tab markers:

2 What are leader dots?

3 What is the purpose of a decimal tab?

4 What are default tabs?

5 What must you remember to do if you want to change a tab setting once you have set it?

Tables

You will learn to

● Create, amend and format tables using the Table facility
● Consider different uses for tables

Like tabs, tables are also used to set out text and numbers in columns, but tables are more flexible. A table is a grid arrangement made up of a series of boxes called cells. These can be printed with or without the gridlines showing and shading or colours can be used to add interest to the table. Continuous text in a table will wordwrap onto the next line within a cell.

Information: Tables

Tables are useful for creating simple forms, minutes of meetings and travel itineraries – in fact any document where information needs to be lined up in columns or rows. They are therefore a quick, easy and efficient way of setting out this type of document so that it is well presented and easy to read. Gridlines automatically appear but these can be removed.

When working with tables it is usual to move across the rows, not down the columns. To move across a table press the Tab key. Text will automatically wrap onto the next line within a cell.

Task 8.1 | Using the Table feature

Method

1   Open a new file.
2   Key in a heading **Countries of the European Union** and press **Enter** twice.
3   Select **Table** menu (wait a few seconds for the full list or click on ⊗ at bottom of menu) – select **Insert**.
4   A further side menu appears – select **Table**.

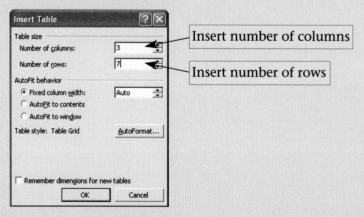

Figure 8.1 Insert Table dialogue box

5   Insert Table dialogue box appears (Figure 8.1).
6   Key in **3** for Number of columns.
7   Key in **7** for Number of rows. Click **OK**.
8   Click into the first box and key in **Country**.
9   Press the **Tab** key to move to the next box and key in **Capital**.
10 Press the **Tab** key and key in **Date of Joining**.
11 Press the **Tab** key which takes you to the next line. Continue to key in the following information. When you reach the end of the table, pressing the **Tab** key produces a new row.

Country	Capital	Date of Joining
Austria	Vienna	1995
Belgium	Brussels	1950
Denmark	Copenhagen	1973
France	Paris	1950
Germany	Berlin	1950
Greece	Athens	1986
Ireland	Dublin	1973
Italy	Rome	1950
Luxembourg	Luxembourg	1950
Netherlands	Amsterdam	1950
Portugal	Lisbon	1986
Spain	Madrid	1986
Sweden	Stockholm	1995
United Kingdom	London	1973

12 Save as **EU Countries** into a new folder called **WP2 Section 8**.
13 Proofread carefully.
14 Format the main heading as size **16** and **bold**.
15 Save.

Information

Tables can also be created by clicking on the **Insert Table** ▦ button and dragging across and down to select the number of rows and columns required (Figure 8.2).

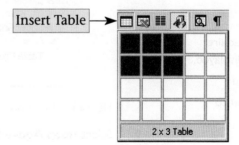

Figure 8.2 Using Insert Table

> ## Information: Modifying tables
>
> Once a table is created it can be changed in a variety of ways, for
> example by adjusting row height and column width, splitting and
> merging cells.

Task 8.2 — Modify a table

Save the document after each change.

Method

Select a row or a column

1　Position the pointer outside the table to the left of the first row and click to highlight the row.
2　Click on **Bold** 𝐁
3　Position the pointer on the top edge of the last column and click to highlight the entire column.
4　Click on **Centre** ≡

Change column width

5　Rest the pointer on the column boundary between **Country** and **Capital** until it changes to ◄‖►. Drag the mouse to the left to reduce the column width to that of the longest line of the text in the column.
6　Repeat for the boundary between **Capital** and **Date of Joining**, and the final boundary.

Change row height

7　Rest the pointer on the row boundary between **Country** and **Austria** until it changes to ≑. (You may need to move the pointer slowly over the boundary until this appears.) Drag the boundary down approximately the height of one row.

Insert a row

8　Click into the **France** row and select **Insert** from the **Table** menu (Figure 8.3).

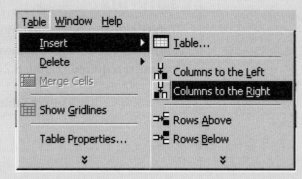

Figure 8.3 Insert row

9　Select **Rows Above** from the side menu.
10　Key in **Finland** in the first cell, **Helsinki** in the second cell and **1995** in the third.

Hint:

Select a cell, row, column or the entire table by choosing **Select** from the **Table** menu and then pick as required.

Hint:

You can also double click the mouse on the column boundary when ◄‖► is visible.

Hint:

To specify a size, click on the required row or column and choose **Table Properties** from the **Table** menu. Click on the **Row** or **Table** tab and specify height or width.

Hint:

If the option you require on a menu is not displayed, click on ⌄ at the bottom of the menu to expand it.

Insert a column

11 Click into the **Country** column and select **Insert** from the **Table** menu (Figure 8.3).

12 Select **Columns to the Right** from the side menu.

13 Key in the heading **Language**.

14 Key in text as follows:

Country	Language
Austria	German
Belgium	Flemish
Denmark	Danish
Finland	Finnish
France	French
Germany	German
Greece	Greek
Ireland	Irish Gaelic
Italy	Italian
Luxembourg	Luxembourgish
Netherlands	Dutch
Portugal	Portuguese
Spain	Spanish
Sweden	Swedish
United Kingdom	English

Merge cells vertically (upwards or downwards)

15 Delete the year alongside **Berlin**.

16 Highlight the **1950** alongside **Paris** and the empty cell below.

17 Select **Merge cells** from the **Table** menu.

18 Repeat for the years alongside **Rome** and **Luxembourg**, and for **Lisbon** and **Madrid**.

Merge cells horizontally (across)

19 Position the cursor in the last cell of the table and press the **Tab** key to create a new row.

20 Drag across the entire row to highlight.

21 Select **Merge cells** from the **Table** menu.

22 Key in:
May 2004 – several more countries join.

Split cells

23 Position the cursor in the last row and select **Split Cells** from the **Table** menu.

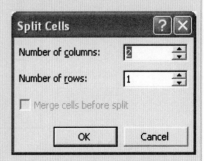

Figure 8.4 Split cells

24 Key in **2** columns and **1** row (these settings are probably already displayed) and click **OK**.

25 In the second cell created, key in:
These are eastern and southern European countries.

Hint:

You can also insert a row using **Insert** from the **Table** menu.

Information: Formatting a table

Once the table is created you can format it by, for example, changing alignments. By applying borders and shading certain parts of a table can be made to stand out.

Task 8.3 | Format a table

Method

Select a cell and vertically align cell content

1 Click inside the left edge of the cell alongside **Paris** and **Berlin** (Figure 8.5) and click to highlight.
2 Select **Table Properties** from the **Table** menu and ensure the **Cell** tab is selected (Figure 8.6).
3 Click on **Center** to centre the contents vertically.
   Click **OK**.

Helsinki	1995
Paris	1950
Berlin	
Athens	1986
Dublin	1973

Figure 8.5 Select a cell

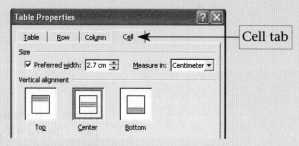 Cell tab

Figure 8.6 Align a cell

Apply shading or colour

4 Select the first row by dragging across it to highlight.
5 Select **Borders and Shading** from the **Format** menu. Ensure the **Shading** tab is selected (Figure 8.7).

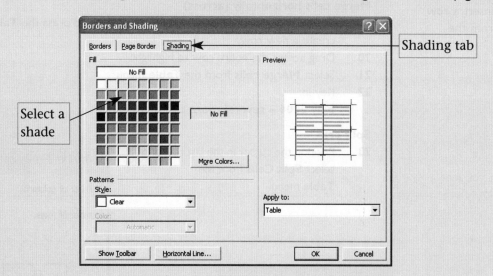 Shading tab

Select a shade

Figure 8.7 Apply shading

6 Select a pale grey colour and click **OK**.
7 Repeat for the last row.

Remove borders

8   Click into the table and select **Borders and Shading** from the **Format** menu (Figure 8.8). Ensure the **Borders** tab is selected.

9   Click on **None** to remove the borders and click **OK**.

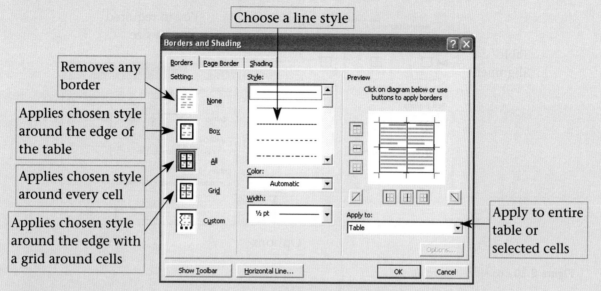

Figure 8.8 Apply borders

Apply borders

10 Click into the table and select **Borders and Shading** from the **Format** menu (Figure 8.8). Notice how any borders will be applied to the entire table – this can be changed by clicking on the drop down arrow under **Apply to:**. Choose a line style from the list (scroll up and down the list if required).

11 Click on **All** to apply the style to all cells and click **OK**.

Apply borders to selected cells

First remove all borders – see **Remove borders** at step 8 above.

12 Highlight the row for Austria and select **Borders and Shading** from the **Format** menu (Figure 8.8). Notice how any borders will be applied to the selected cell(s).

13 Choose a line style and click on **Box**. Click **OK**.

14 Repeat for the two other countries that were last to join in 1995.

Delete a row or column

15 Click in the last row and select **Delete** from the **Table** menu (Figure 8.9).

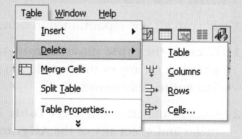

Figure 8.9 Delete row/column

16 Select **Rows** from the side menu that appears.

17 Click in the last column and select **Delete** from the **Table** menu.

18 Select **Columns** from the side menu that appears. **Print preview** and notice how the side border has disappeared with the column.

19 Add borders to the entire table – see **Apply Borders** at step 10 above.

Adjust the margin inside cells

20   Click inside the table and select **Table Properties** from the **Table** menu. Click on **Options** (Figure 8.10).

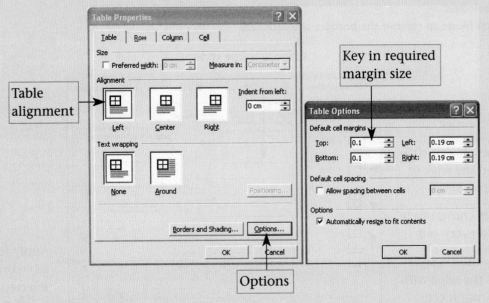

Figure 8.10 Change cell margins

21   In **Table Options** key in **0.1** for each margin, top, bottom, left and right.
22   Click **OK**, then **OK** again.

Reposition a table
Ensure you are in **Print Layout View** (**View** menu – **Print Layout**).
23   Rest the cursor on the table until the table move handle appears
      at the top left corner of the table (Figure 8.11).
24   Rest the pointer on this handle, and a four-headed arrow appears.
25   Drag the table down the page a little and across to the middle.
26   Add your name in the footer.
27   Save the file and print.

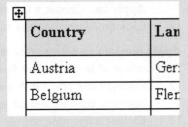

Figure 8.11 Table move handle

Hint:

The small square handle that appears at the bottom right of the table at the same time can be used to resize the table.

Remember:

You can also select a cell, row, column or the entire table by choosing **Select** from the **Table** menu and then pick as required.

Things to do

A table can also be repositioned in other ways – try each of these now.

1   Click on the **table move handle** to select/highlight the table and click on any of the text alignment buttons, e.g. **Centre** ≣. The entire table moves.

2   Click in the table and select **Table Properties** from the **Table** menu and select any of the **Alignment** options – see Figure 8.10 above. The entire table moves.

And finally ...
You may like to experiment with **Table Autoformat** on the **Table** menu.

Things to do

1 Think about the different uses you could put tables to.
2 Create a 3-column table with the days of the week down the first column, the lessons on each day in the second column and the room numbers in the third. If you are not a student, key in the things you normally do on each day of the week and where you do them.

Information: An itinerary

An **itinerary** is a plan of travel, a tour or journey giving information such as dates, times and destinations. In the next task (Practise your skills 8.1) you will create an itinerary for a trip to Australia.

→ Practise your skills 8.1

1 Open a new document and set the page up as **A4 portrait** with margins of **3 cm** top, bottom, left and right.

2 Insert a **3** column table with **8** rows and key in the following:

Day 1	London – Melbourne	City tour 2 days free
Day 4	Melbourne – Adelaide via the Great Ocean Road	3 days Tantanoola Caves Mt Gambier
Day 7	Adelaide – Perth by air	Fremantle Kangaroo Island 1 free day
Day 10	Perth – Alice Springs by air	Gateway to Central Australia Desert Park
Day 12	Alice Springs – Uluru (Ayers Rock)	Outback overnight experience
Day 13	Uluru – Cairns by air	Great Barrier Reef 2 day coastal break
Day 16	Cairns – Sydney by air	Sydney Opera House Harbour Bridge 2 days free
Day 19	Sydney – London	

3 Save the document as **Itinerary** into the **WP2 Skills Practice** folder.
4 Insert a row above the first row and merge the cells of this row together.
5 In this new row key in **The Australian Experience**.
6 Split this row into **2 columns** and key in **19 Day Escorted Tour**.
7 Change the text in the first row to **bold**, size **16** and **centre** it.

8 Add light grey shading to the first row.

9 Change the height of the first row to approximately twice its original height.

10 Adjust the width of the first of the three main columns to fit the text.

11 Adjust the second column width as you feel fit.

12 Change the font throughout to **Arial**.

13 Change the border around the edge of the table to a **double line style** with the **Grid Setting**. (Use the first **double line** style with a $\frac{1}{2}$**pt width**.)

14 Use the move handle to move the table part way down the page.

15 Proofread, spellcheck (adding any names to the dictionary) and print preview.

16 Save and print.

→ Practise your skills 8.2

1 Open a document, **A4 portrait** with margins of **3 cm** top, bottom, left and right.

2 Key in the two lines of text as follows, leaving a line space between them:

   Working with tables

   Tick which skills you have achieved.

3 Create a **3** column table with **15** rows and key in text as shown:

Skills checklist		Tick here
1	Select a row	
2	Change column width	
3	Change row height	
4	Insert a row	
5	Merge cells vertically	
6	Merge cells horizontally	
7	Change cell alignment	
8	Apply shading	
9	Remove borders	
10	Apply borders	
11	Delete a row/column	
12	Adjust cell margins	
13	Reposition a table	
All skills achieved		

4 Save the file as **Working with tables** into the **WP2 Skills Practice** folder.

5 Merge the first two cells in the first row together.

6 Repeat for the last row.

7 Reduce the width of all columns to fit the data in them.

8 Increase the height of the first row to approximately double it.

9 Repeat for the last row.

10 Apply a light grey shade to the first row and the last row.

11 Vertically align the contents of the first and last rows to the centre of the cell.

12 Insert a row above the row numbered 1 and below the row numbered 13.

13 Remove borders from the table.

14 Apply borders to the cells in the third column of the *numbered rows only*.

15 Apply a border to the last cell in the last row.

16 Embolden the main heading and change to size **16**.

17 Embolden text in the shaded rows.

18 Above the table, centre the heading and the line below.

19 Use the move handle to move the table across to the centre of the page.

20 Proofread and spellcheck.

21 Save with your name and the filename in the footer and print.

Things to do

1 Now you should complete this checklist! If there are any gaps in your skills, refer back to the instructions in this section and practice.

2 Draw a rough sketch on blank paper of an itinerary for a visitor coming to stay with you or your company for a few days, listing some of the places they might visit during their stay. Then produce the itinerary as a table.

→ Check your knowledge

1 When might you use tables in documents?

2 Why are tables so useful?

3 Why might you use borders and shading on a table?

4 What is an itinerary?

Consolidation 2

1 Open a new **A5 portrait** page with left and right margins of **2 cm** and create the following:

Summer Fete

The summer fete will take place this year on 14th June. Your help is always appreciated in making this occasion a great success and hopefully we will raise funds towards a new swimming pool cover. Please indicate below if you are able to help.

	Setting up	Entrance/ Car Park	Manning a stall	Clearing up
10–12				
2–3				
3–4				
4–5				

Name...

Child's name...

Class..

Please return this page to your child's teacher.

2 Proofread and check, save as **Fete** into **Consolidation** folder and print.

3 Open the file **Activity Day** from the **Consolidation** folder.

4 Save it as **Activity Day Version 2**.

5 Delete **Warren First School** from the heading.

6 Change the left and right margins to **2.75 cm**.

7 Change the page number to start at **1**.

8 Delete the page number in the footer and replace it with **Page X of Y** to show the total number of pages.

9 Change the numbering to bullets.

10 Delete the dotted line across the page and in its place set a dashed line leader tab at **15 cm**.

11 Key in **Cut here** and press the Tab key to create a broken line.

12 On the line reading **Child's name**, create a solid line leader tab at **10 cm**. Press the Tab key after **name** to produce the line.

13 Highlight the list of activities at the bottom of the page and create after each paragraph spacing of **12 pt**.

14 Insert a page break at the bottom of the page.

15 Copy the content of the file **Fete** and paste into **Activity Day Version 2** on the new page.

16 Proofread, check the layout carefully, adjust if necessary. Print preview.

17 Save and print.

18 Use **Save As** to save a copy of the document onto floppy disk, into a new folder called **Backup**, and close.

Section 9

Templates and business documents

You will learn to

- Use existing templates
- Create templates
- Insert WordArt
- Consider features of commonly used documents – memos, letters, fax cover sheets, reports and invoices

A template is a file that already holds the basic structure of a document, ready for you to use over and over again. This might include the layout and any formatting, graphics and text as well. For example, you may have a standard letter stored as a template. When you open up a file based on the template (in other words a copy of it), you can then complete it without having to recreate it from the beginning. This obviously saves a lot of time and it also ensures that a standard layout is used every time. You will look at different types of document in this section and you should also have your collected documents ready to look at. Your tutor may also have some samples. These documents were covered in Level 1.

Information: Memos

A memo is a form of communication used within an organisation and is usually entirely word processed but may sometimes be handwritten on a prepared memo form. (You created both of these in Level 1.) They are less formal than business letters. Do you have any memos in the documents you have gathered? If so, see how they compare with documents you are now going to produce. Word has memo templates already set up for you to use.

Task 9.1 Use a memo template

Method

1   Create a new folder and call it **WP2 Section 9**.
2   Select **New** from the **File** menu and click on **General Templates** in the **Task pane** (Figure 9.1).

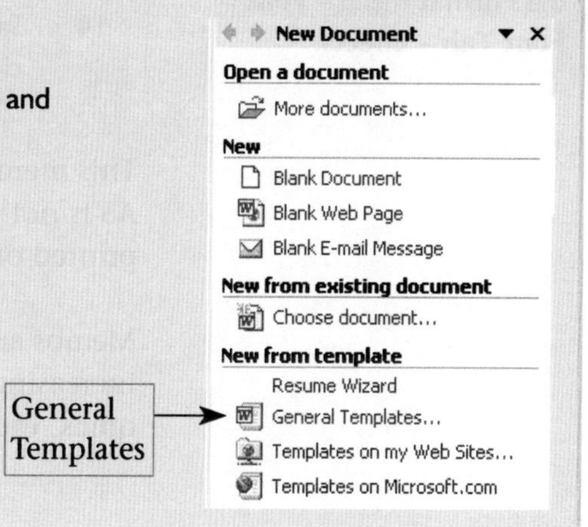

Figure 9.1 General templates

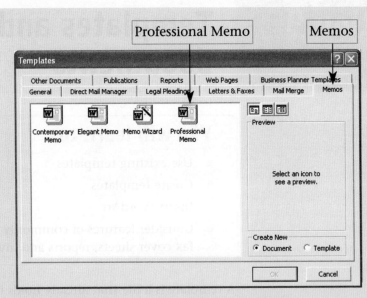

Figure 9.2 Memo templates

3   Select the **Memos tab** from the Templates window, click on **Professional Memo** and then click **OK** (Figure 9.2).

4   Highlight the text in the top right corner that reads **Company name here** and key in **Pullman plc**.

5   Click alongside **To**: in the text that reads **[Click here and type name]** and key in **Sinead O'Malley**.

6   Click alongside **From**: in the text that reads **[Click here and type name]** and key in your name.

7   Click alongside **cc.** in the text that reads **[Click here and type name]** and key in **Jonah Pullman.**

8   Notice how today's date is already inserted automatically.

9   Click alongside **Re**: in the text that reads **[Click here and type subject]** and key in **Sales Meeting**.

10   Highlight and delete the text below the horizontal line.

11   Position the cursor below the line (you may need to press **Enter**) and key in: **The next Sales Meeting will take place on 6th December and all Regional Sales Managers will be attending together with Area Managers. The marketing strategy for the next six months will be announced at this meeting and it would be very useful if you could come along with your team to present your part in these plans. Please let me know as soon as possible how many people you are likely to bring with you.**

12   Proofread and spellcheck.

13   Remove the page number from the footer.

14   Save the memo as **Sales** memo into the **WP2 Section 9 folder**, print and close.

This memo is only short and would fit onto A5 paper. However, in practice A5 is not generally used for business documents as most documents are printed only on A4.

Memos are not used as much as they used to be, as e-mail has become increasingly popular for this type of internal communication because it is so quick, easy and instant.

Information: Business letters

Business letters are formal documents used as an external form of communication. That is to say, they are sent to persons outside an organisation, such as to clients. This is often the only contact a client has with the organisation and therefore it is important that the impression given is a professional one. This can be done by making sure the letter is accurate and well-presented. Letters follow a very similar layout although most organisations have their own preferred **housestyle** which might include a specific layout, font and style. They would be prepared on A4 portrait paper with equal margins on the left and right, and usually follow the **fully blocked style** where each line starts at the left-hand margin.

You will hopefully have collected some examples of letters. Look at them now to see what similar features they may have. They will probably all have a logo, contact details such as address, telephone and fax number, e-mail address, and certainly a date. A subject heading is usually included. They might have a website address and if they are a large organisation they may also have a registered office address. Are your letters all in the fully blocked style? If other documents were sent with a letter you will probably see Enc at the bottom indicating an enclosure. Can you identify the fonts used? Look at the example letter in Figure 9.3.

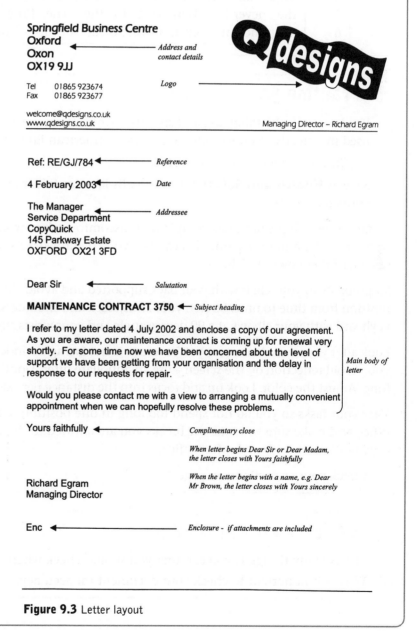

Figure 9.3 Letter layout

→ Practise your skills 1

Proofread the following text and note down the line number and word/s of any errors you spot where **B** differs from the original **A**. There are 12 errors to spot. Check your findings on page 84.

A	
1	The Norwegian holiday promised a cruise around fjords in and out around the
2	small islands and calling at picture-postcard fishing villages and deserted bays.
3	The scenery showed a marked contrast between the breathtaking mountains
4	and the little colourful villages. There was also the chance to make the never-
5	forgotten visit to the 'The Kingdom of the Whales' to see magnificent black
6	and white orcas. All this – 7 days and 6 nights for only £475.

B	
1	The Norwegian holiday promised a cruise around fiords in and out around the
2	the small islands and calling at picture postcard fishing villages and deserted
3	bays. The scenery shows a market contrast between the breath-taking
4	mountains and the little colorful villages. There was also the chance to make
5	the never-forgotten visit to the 'The Kingdom for the Wales' to see
6	magnificient black and white orcas. All this – 7 days and nights for only £473.

→ Practise your skills 2

1 Read through the following and spot the errors. There are 10 in total – 8 words correctly spelt but used incorrectly, 1 punctuation error and 1 American English word.

2 Key in the correct version of the file.

3 Save as **Health and Safety** into the Skills Practice folder and print. On your printout mark the corrected words.

Some people using computers complain of discomfort when working, such as soar hands and eyes, or back, shoulder and neck pain. This can be avoided and workers must be aware of what they can do to safeguard there own health.

Sit probably in your chair with your back supported and avoid sitting in a twisted position. Change position from time to time. Stretch your arms, neck and shoulders. Hands should be raised above the keyboard with your elbows at a 90 degree angle and your wrists should be straight, fingers curled slightly.

Look after your eyes. Make sure you're screen is not facing a window or the window is directly behind you. Avoid reflection on the screen – use an anti-glare filter. Dont' look at the screen to intensely fore too long. Adjust the color. Look up and focus into the distance periodically and ensure you blink your eyes.

Vary your tasks so you do not spend too long in one position. Get up from your desk, walk round the office and make sure you take the breaks you are entitled to. If you need advise, cheque with your organisation's health and safety officer.

4 Check your corrections on page 84.

→ Check your knowledge

1 List as many things as you can that you should check when proofreading.

2 Why is it important to check your document for accuracy, correctness and meaning?

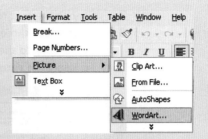

Figure 9.4 Insert WordArt

Choose WordArt style

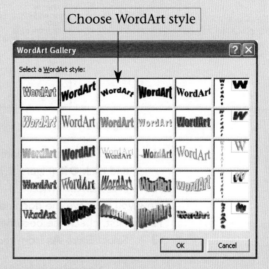

Figure 9.5 WordArt Gallery

3   Choose WordArt style as indicated in Figure 9.5 and click **OK**.
4   Key in **Pullman plc** (Figure 9.6) and click **OK**. WordArt appears with handles on the sides and corners.

Figure 9.6 Enter WordArt text

5   Position the pointer over the words of the logo until the pointer changes to a four-headed arrow ✛. Then drag it to the top middle of the page.
6   Key in the contact details:
Barrington Park
Upper Causeway
Oxon
OX21 4PH
Tel: 01637 224475 Fax: 01637 224476
www.pullmanplc.co.uk
enquiries @pullmanplc.co.uk

7   Change the font to **Arial** and **centre** under the company name.

8   Press **Enter** three times and click on the **Align Left** button to bring the cursor back to the margin.

9   To insert the date – select **Date and Time** from the **Insert** menu.

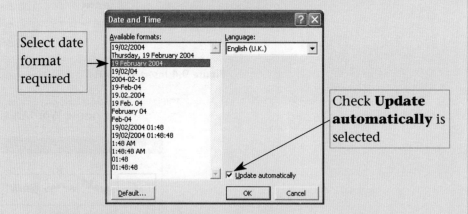

Select date format required

Check **Update automatically** is selected

Figure 9.7 Insert date

10   Select the required date format, check **Update automatically** is selected and click **OK** (Figure 9.7).

11   Press **Enter** twice.

Now you will save the document as a template.

12   First, check the document very carefully.

13   Select **Save As** from the **File** menu (Figure 9.8).

Save in: box changes automatically to **Templates** when file type Document Template is selected

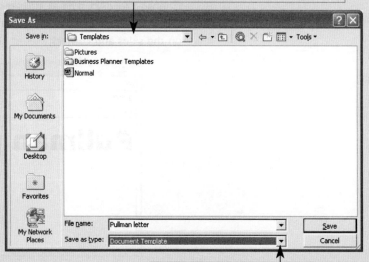

Select **Document Template** as the file type from the drop down list

Figure 9.8 Save as a template

14   Key in the filename **Pullman Letter**.

15   Click on the drop down arrow alongside the **Save as type:** box and select **Document Template**. Notice that the **Save in:** box automatically changes to **Templates**.

16   Click on **Save** and close the document.

Hint:

The Templates folder is where all templates are automatically stored. This folder is part of Word's program file structure – it depends on your setup as to where this is located.

Method

1   Select **New** from the **File** menu and click on **General Templates** in the **Task pane**.

2   On the **General** tab click on **Pullman Letter** to open a copy of the template. Notice that there is no filename in the title bar at the top of the window, only a document number. This is because you are using a copy of the original template.

3   Click below the date ensuring you leave a clear line and key in the following:
Ms P Templeton
14 Leyton Street
Bicester
Oxon
OX24 9HG

4   Press **Enter** twice and key in **Dear Ms Templeton**.

5   Press **Enter** twice, key in **ADMINISTRATION ASSISTANT** and embolden it.

6   Press **Enter** twice and key in:
Thank you for your recent application for the above position. We are pleased to inform you that you have been shortlisted for interview and we invite you to attend on Tuesday 4th March at 10.30 am. On arrival at reception, please ask for Sinead Donnelly.

We enclose a map of our location and look forward to meeting you.

Yours sincerely

7   Press **Enter** five times to leave space for a signature and key in:
Pierre Blanc
Human Resources Assistant

8   Press **Enter** twice and key in **Enc** to indicate an enclosure.

9   Check the document, save as **Job letter** into the **WP2 Section 9** folder, print and close.

Hint:

Notice how no punctuation is used in the address, salutation or complimentary close, only in the body of the letter.

Hint:

If you use a name in the salutation, e.g. Dear Miss Jones, use Yours sincerely for the complimentary close. For Dear Sir/Dear Madam, use Yours faithfully.

Information: Fax cover sheets

These are completed and sent by fax with or without accompanying documents. They would be completed entirely by word processing if sent directly from a computer but may be filled in by hand if using a fax machine. You created a fax cover sheet for Level 1. To look at an example now, select **New** from the **File** menu and click on **General Templates** in the **Task pane**. Select **Professional Fax** from the **Letters & Faxes** tab. Print this out. Fax sheets are likely to be on A4 portrait paper with equal margins on the left and right. Fax is an abbreviation for facsimile – which means a copy.

Task 9.5 — Create a fax cover sheet template

For this task you will use a copy of the Pullman letter template and modify it to create a fax template.

Method

1. Select **New** from the **File** menu and click on **General Templates** in the **Task pane**.
2. On the **General** tab, click on **Pullman Letter**.
3. Delete the date and key in **FAX** in its place, size **36** and **bold**.
4. Press **Enter** twice and insert a table consisting of 2 columns and 6 rows.
5. In the first column of each row, key in the following:
   To
   Fax No
   From
   Date
   Subject
   No of pages including cover sheet
6. In the cell alongside Date, insert the date to update automatically.
7. Below the table, key in **Message** and press **Enter**. Embolden the word **Message**.
8. Check carefully and save as **Pullman Fax**, ensuring that **Document Template** is selected in the **Save as:** box.
9. Close the new template.

Hint:

It is important to include the total number of pages so that the recipient can check to ensure they receive all pages.

Remember:

Templates save automatically to a Templates folder.

Task 9.6 — Use the new fax cover sheet template

Method

1. Select **New** from the **File** menu and click on **General Templates** in the **Task pane**.
2. On the **General** tab, click on **Pullman Letter**.
3. Fill in the fax form details as below:

To	Emile Barthez
Fax No	01637 786576
From	Your name
Date	Today's date
Subject	New Product Range
No of pages including cover sheet	1

4. Key in the message:
   Just to confirm that the launch of the New Product Range will go ahead as planned on the 10th of next month. Could you please let me know how many colleagues will be attending?
5. Check, save as **New product range fax** into the **WP2 Section 9** folder and print.
6. Close.

Information: Reports

Reports may be written at regular intervals to give information, such as a monthly progress report comparing the house sales of each branch of an estate agency. This type of **information report** would be factual and might be **informal** (Figure 9.9). An **investigation report** would be more **formal**. In the next task you will create a template for an investigation report with the section headings you would be likely to see and then use a copy of it to explain them.

Report on February House Sales – Southern Region

Overview

The market improved in the New Year following the usual trends. However, sales were not as good as for the same period over the past three years due to the downturn in the economy. There have not been so many purchasers looking to buy-to-let at the lower end of the market which has slowed down sales locally.

Reading

There were 28 new instructions during the month and offers were made on 38 properties. Completions totalled 35. The office had been awarded the contract to sell the new Watergate development of 154 mixed properties.

Newbury

Newbury took 25 new instructions and 22 offers were made. Nineteen completions took place. Business has suffered due to special rate opening offers made by a newly-opened competitor, but it was significant that some of their clients were now coming to us as the response had not been as expected.

Hungerford

This month saw 24 new instructions and 29 offers. Twenty-five sales were completed which was particularly good for this small branch. This was partly due to a new release of first-time buyer properties on the Marchwind development.

Monthly Figures

Figures for the region are:

	Reading	Newbury	Hungerford
New instructions	28	25	24
Offers	38	22	29
Completions	35	19	25

With the market as it is currently, we cannot afford to be complacent. We have always prided ourselves on our reputation, but if there are fewer buyers out there, it is up to us to make sure that the quality of service we offer both to our client house-owners and to prospective purchasers is second to none.

John Lloyd
Regional Sales Manager

Figure 9.9 Example of an informal report

Task 9.7 — Create a report template

Method

1. Open a new document and key in the following pressing **Enter** *four times* after each line:
   Report on
   Introduction
   Method
   Findings
   Recommendations

2. Make each heading bold and size 14 – do each separately as you want the lines between to be of normal size when you come to use them.

3. Save the document as a template with the name **Formal Report** and close it.

Task 9.8 — Use the new report template

Method

1. Select **New** from the **File** menu and click on **General Templates** in the **Task pane**.
2. On the **General** tab, click on **Formal report**.
   In the space below **Report on**, key in:
   This is where the subject of the report goes. It might read, for example, Report on the Feasibility of Opening a New Branch Office in Wokingham. A feasibility study is one which investigates whether or not something is possible or practical.
3. Below **Introduction**, key in:
   This section sets the scene and describes what the report is about, who has commissioned or requested it and when it should be completed by.
4. Below **Method**, key in:
   The Method section describes how the investigation was carried out. In this example it might include surveying the local market, finding out how many other agents exist, how long they have been established, costs of commercial premises, looking at trends of house prices in local papers, carrying out market research interviews on the public.
5. Below **Findings**, key in:
   This is probably self-explanatory and would list in detail what had been found out as a result of investigations carried out.
6. Below **Recommendations**, key in:
   This section sets out what is recommended following the Findings. In this example it might suggest carrying out further investigations and delaying any decisions for, say, another year. It might recommend a new branch or it might not. Another name for this section might be Conclusions.
7. Check your work.
8. Save the document as **Formal Report Features** into the **WP2 Section 9** folder and print.

Information: Invoices

An invoice is rather like a bill which states how much money is owed for services provided or goods ordered. In the business world when a company orders goods, say roofing materials ordered by a building company, the suppliers will deliver the goods and send an invoice stating what was delivered and how much is owed. An estate agent would send an invoice to a client setting out how much their bill was for services provided in selling a house.

An example of an invoice is shown in Figure 9.10. Note the information included, such as the **invoice number** and **order number**, **description of items** and **VAT** (Value Added Tax). **E & OE** at the bottom stands for Errors and Omissions Excepted, which means that the information contained in the invoice was produced in good faith and if there are any errors, the amounts due may be subject to amendment. **Terms: 30 days** indicates that the invoice should be paid within 30 days.

Invoices may be produced on A4 paper, portrait or landscape, or two-thirds A4 size. An invoice is often created using a spreadsheet program. Do you have any sample invoices to compare with this one? →

Pullman plc

Barrington Park
Upper Causeway
Oxon
OX21 4PH
Tel: 01637 224475 Fax: 01637 224476
www.pullmanplc.co.uk
enquiries@pullmanplc.co.uk

4 February 2004

INVOICE
VAT Registration no 123/6789

To:

Manic Mobiles
Lower Causeway
Oxon
OX22 7QT

Invoice no	Despatch Date	Your order no.
6675	4/2/04	MM349

Item	Code	Quantity	Price	Total Price
Galaxy Handset	GH1	12	£44.95	£539.40
Venus Handset	VH5	10	£53.75	£537.50
			Sub Total	£1076.90
			Delivery	£15.00
			VAT	£191.08
			TOTAL DUE	£1282.98

E & OE
Terms: 30 days

Figure 9.10 Example of an invoice

→ Practise your skills 9.1

1 Sketch on blank paper the memo template you will create by following the steps in this task before you actually create it.

2 Create a memo template for A4 size paper with margins left and right of **3 cm**.

3 Insert the word **Memo** as WordArt in the top middle of the page.

4 Set a left tab at **3 cm**.

5 Key in **To:** at the margin and press the **Tab** key. Press **Enter** twice.

6 Key in **From:** at the margin and press the **Tab** key. Press **Enter** twice.

7 Key in **Date:** at the margin and press the **Tab** key.

8 To insert the date – select **Date and Time** from the **Insert** menu (Figure 9.7) and select the required date format, check **Update automatically** is selected and click **OK**.

9 Press **Enter** twice.

10 Key in **Subject:** at the margin and press the **Tab** key. Press **Enter** twice.

11 Check carefully and save as **Simple A4 memo** ensuring that **Document Template** is selected in the **Save as:** box.

12 Close the new template.

13 Using **File – New** and **General Templates** from the **Task pane**, select the new template and produce a memo to send to your tutor or employer telling them you will be absent next Tuesday morning due to a dental appointment.

14 Save with a suitable name into the **WP2 Skills Practice** folder, print and close.

→ Practise your skills 9.2

1 Create another similar memo template, this time for **A5 landscape** with margins all round (top, bottom, left and right) of **2 cm**.

2 Check it and save as **Simple A5 memo**. Ensure that **Document Template** is selected in the **Save as:** box. Close the template file.

3 Use a copy of it to send to a colleague or another student telling them that you can attend the meeting on Friday.

4 Proofread, spellcheck (adding any names to the dictionary) and print preview. Save with a suitable name into the **WP2 Skills Practice** folder and print.

→ Practise your skills 9.3

1 Sketch on blank paper the letter template you will create by following the steps in this task before you create it.

2 Create an A4 letter template with your home address aligned to the right.

3 Press **Enter** twice and insert the date as you did above so that it updates automatically. Align this date to the left.

4 Press **Enter** twice and key in **Addressee**. This will remind you to key in the addressee's name and address when you use the template.

5 Press **Enter** twice and key in **Dear**.

6 Press **Enter** four times and key in **Yours sincerely**.

7 Press **Enter** once and key in **Yours faithfully**. When you use the template you can delete whichever complimentary close is not required.

8 Press **Enter** five times and key in your name.

9 Check carefully and save as **Personal letter** and ensure that **Document Template** is selected in the **Save as:** box. Close the template file.

10 Using **File – New** and **General Templates** from the **Task pane**, open a copy of this template. You are going to send a letter to a friend telling them briefly about the course you are following.

11 Delete the word **Addressee** and key in your friend's name and address.

12 Key in your friend's name after Dear.

Remember:

The complimentary close is the way that a letter is finished, e.g. Yours sincerely.

→

13 Position the cursor one clear line space below Dear and compose your letter.

14 Delete Yours faithfully. As your letter is to a friend, key in **Best wishes** on the line before Yours sincerely to make it sound less formal.

15 Proofread, spellcheck (adding any names to the dictionary) and print preview.

16 Save with a suitable name into the **WP2 Skills Practice** folder and print.

→ Practise your skills 9.4

1 Reproduce the invoice shown in Figure 9.9 above using a copy of the Pullman letter template. Notice how two tables and borders have been used. Note too how the prices all show two places after the decimal point and have been aligned to the right so the decimal points are lined up.

2 Check the document, save as **Manic Mobiles invoice** and print.

3 Now convert this document to a template. First, delete the information that would not be correct to send to another customer. The date will update automatically so this can stay. The address of the customer should be deleted and all the information in the two tables not in bold, leaving just the headings.

4 Check carefully and save as **Pullman invoice**, ensuring that **Document Template** is selected in the **Save as:** box. Close the template file.

5 Using **File – New** and **General Templates** from the **Task pane**, open a copy of this template. Send an invoice to yourself as the customer, making up the items and prices.

Things to do

1 Print a blank copy of the fax template and fill in by hand the same information as used in Task 9.6 above.

2 Design a fax cover sheet on blank paper that you could use to send a fax from yourself.

3 Print a copy of the Pullman A5 memo and fill it in by hand using the same information as used in Practise your skills 9.2.

→ Check your knowledge

1 What is a template and what is the advantage of using one?

2 What is a housestyle?

3 What is the fully blocked style?

4 If you use a person's name in the salutation of a letter, e.g. Dear Mr Joynson, the letter closes with Yours faithfully. True or False?

5 Name two types of report.

6 What is an invoice?

Section 10 | Styles

You will learn to

- Apply styles to text
- Edit styles
- Create styles

Styles are a quick way of applying formats to text and ensuring consistency throughout a document. Word has several styles already created but you can also set up your own. As an example, you might want to format all your main headings in a particular way so they all look the same – so you create a style and apply it to each heading. Any text with a style applied to it becomes 'tagged' with that style. Then if you want to change the style, for example to another font, you just change the style once and every piece of text tagged with that style will change automatically. Styles can be created for Paragraphs, Characters, Tables and Lists.

Task 10.1 | Apply styles

In this task you will apply Word's default styles to a document. Locate **Styles** to the left of the **Font** list on the Formatting toolbar and click on the arrow alongside it to see a list of styles. (See Figure 10.1. Your list of styles may be slightly different.) Press **Esc** (Escape) in the top left corner of the keyboard to close the list.

Method

1 Open the file **Buying a Conservatory** from My Documents.
2 Position the cursor in the first heading **So you want a Conservatory?**
3 Click on the drop down arrow alongside the **Styles** box (Figure 10.1) and click on **Heading 2**. The formatting of the heading should change.
4 Position the cursor in the subheading **What is a conservatory?** and select **Heading 3** from the styles list.
5 Repeat for the remaining two subheadings, selecting the style **Heading 3.**

Styles can also be selected from the Styles and Formatting Task pane which opens by clicking on the Styles and Formatting ⏁ button. Click on this now. (Figure 10.1).

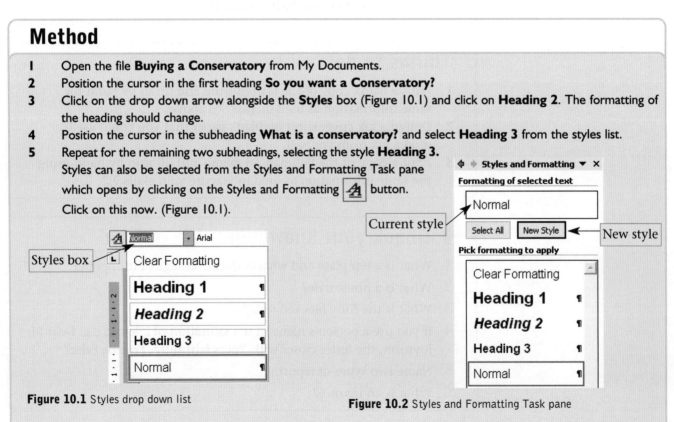

Figure 10.1 Styles drop down list

Figure 10.2 Styles and Formatting Task pane

Task 10.2	Edit styles – font options

Method

1   Position the mouse pointer over **Heading 2** in the Task pane and click on the drop down arrow that appears (Figure 10.3).

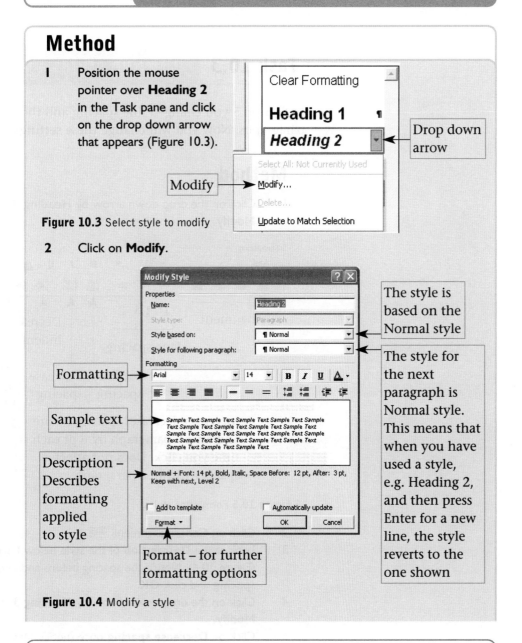

Figure 10.3 Select style to modify

2   Click on **Modify**.

Figure 10.4 Modify a style

3	In the formatting row seen in the middle of Figure 10.4, click on the drop down list of fonts and choose **Tahoma**, then size 16 and **bold**.
4	Click **OK**. Notice how the first heading changes.
5	Repeat numbers 1 and 2 above, selecting **Heading 3** from the Task pane.
6	Change the font to **Tahoma**, size **14**, **bold** and click **OK**. The sub headings should change.
7	Repeat this process selecting the style **Normal**.
8	Change the font to **Tahoma**, size **11** and click **OK**. The remaining text should change.
9	Save the document.

Task 10.3   Change styles – paragraph options

In Section 5 you changed line spacing and the spacing before and after paragraphs. Now you will change these settings in a style.

Method

1	Click on the drop down arrow by **Heading 2** in the Task pane and select **Modify**.

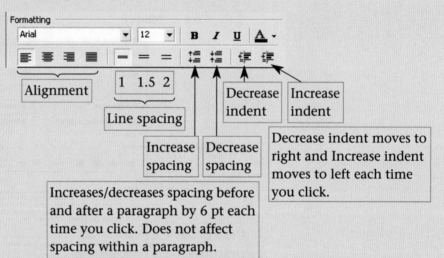

Figure 10.5 Formatting styles

2	Click on **Centre** alignment ≡.
3	Look at the **Description** of the style below Formatting and Sample text (Figure 10.4). Notice the spacing before and after. Click on **Decrease spacing** and click **OK**.
4	Click on the drop down arrow by **Heading 3** in the Task pane and select **Modify**.
5	Click on **Decrease spacing** once (notice Description) and then again. Click **OK**.
6	Click on the drop down arrow by **Normal** in the Task pane and select **Modify**.
7	Click on **1.5 line spacing** and click **OK**.
8	Save, print and close the document.

> **Information:** Creating new styles
>
> There are two ways of creating new styles: one by using the Styles dialogue windows as above, the other by creating **Styles by Example**, which is the quickest way.

Task 10.4 | Create new styles 1

Method

1   Open a new file and key in the following using outline numbering:
    Seasons
    1. Spring
        1.1. February
        1.2. March
        1.3. April
    2. Summer
        2.1. May
        2.2. June
        2.3. July
        2.4. August
    3. Autumn
        3.1. September
        3.2. October
    4. Winter
        4.1. November
        4.2. December
        4.3. January

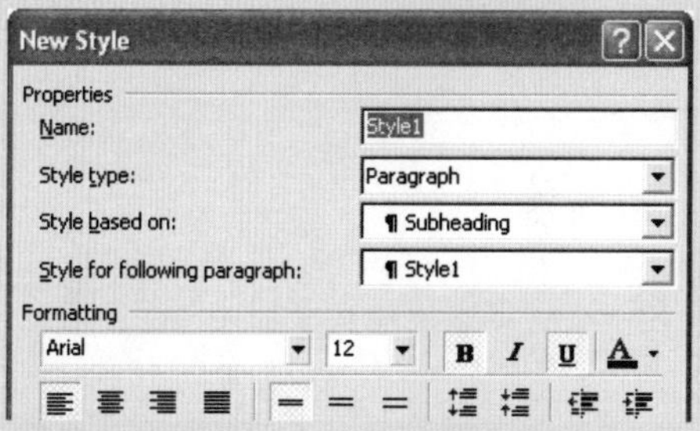

Figure 10.6 Create a new style

2   Click on **New Style** | New Style | in the Styles and Formatting Task pane.
3   Key in the Name **Main heading** and select the following settings:

    Style type   Paragraph
    Style based on   Normal
    Style for following paragraph   Normal

4   Set the font as **Arial**, size **18**, **Bold** and **Underlined**.
5   Click twice on **Increase Paragraph spacing** (giving 12 pt before and after) and click **OK**.
6   Click on the heading **Seasons** and click on **Main heading** in the Styles Task pane.
7   Save the file as **Seasons** into **My Documents**.

Hint:

You can also create Character, Table and List styles.

Hint:

To set paragraph spacing as other than 6 pt increments, click on the **Format** button in the bottom left corner of the Modify style dialogue window and select **Paragraph**.

Task 10.5   Create new styles 2 (style by example)

With this method you first apply formatting to text and then create a style from it. To do this you will use the Styles dropdown list on the Formatting toolbar.

Method

1. Click in the paragraph numbered 1. (Spring). Select **Paragraph** from the **Format** menu and change the spacing before and after the paragraph to **18 pt**.
2. With the cursor still in this text, click into the style name box ![icon] main item ▼ and with the existing style name highlighted, key in **Main item**. Press **Enter**.
3. Click into the paragraph numbered 2 and select **Main item** style from either the drop down list or the task pane.
4. Repeat for the paragraphs numbered 3 and 4.
5. Click in the paragraph numbered 1.1. and change the spacing before and after the paragraph to **6 pt**.
6. With the cursor still in this text, click into the style name box and, with the existing style name highlighted, key in **Sub item**. Press **Enter**.
7. Apply this new style to all the paragraphs numbered 1.2., 1.3. etc.
8. Add your name to the footer, save and print.

Information:

The styles you have used are **Paragraph styles**, which means that they are applied to the entire paragraph in which the cursor sits. If you create **Character styles** you would need to highlight text before applying the style.

Whenever you apply any manual formatting to text, it appears in the task pane list. You can choose to display only styles and/or formatting by selecting from the **Show:** box at the bottom of the task pane.

→ Practise your skills 10.1

1. Open the file **Activity Day version 2** from the **Backup folder** on floppy disk. (You should also have a copy in the Consolidation folder.)
2. Create a new style called **Main headings** and format this style as **Arial**, bold, size **16**.
3. Apply the new style to the heading at the top of each page.
4. Create another new style called **List items** and format this style as **Arial, bold**, size **12**.
5. Apply the **List items** style to Badminton, Swimming, Football and Tennis in the top half of the page.
6. Save the file as **Activity Day version 3** into the **Backup folder** on the floppy disk.
7. Save another copy into the **Consolidation** folder. Print and close.

→ Practise your skills 10.2

Here you will create a style by example.

1 Open the document **Minutes** from the **WP2 Skills Practice** folder.
2 Highlight the paragraph item **1. Minutes of the last meeting** and using **Paragraph** from the **Format** menu, change the spacing after the paragraph to **6 pt**.
3 Highlight the formatted text (if not already highlighted) and create a style by example, calling the style **Minutes item**.
4 Apply the style to the other main items.
5 Format the paragraph numbered **2.1** with a space after of **4 pt**.
6 Create a new style using the style by example method and call it **Sub item**.
7 Use this new **Sub item** style to format the paragraphs numbered 2.2, 3.1, 3.2, 3.3, 4.1, 4.2, 5.1, 5.2, and 5.3.
8 Save the document as **Minutes version 2** into the **WP2 Skills Practice** folder, print and close.

→ Check your knowledge

1 What are the advantages of using styles?
2 How is a style applied?
3 What is creating a style by example?
4 What style is text automatically formatted as, unless another style has been applied?

You will learn to

- Insert clip art
- Arrange and group graphical elements
- Insert graphical shapes
- Insert a photographic image
- Apply text wrapping
- Insert a chart
- Change character spacing
- Insert symbols

Hint:

Position the mouse pointer over any button without clicking and a screen tip will appear to explain its purpose.

Graphics, in the form of clip art and images, are used to illustrate and improve the appearance of a document. These were used in Level 1, as were other graphical features – WordArt, also used in Section 9, and symbols. In this section you will revise these features and also insert graphical shapes and charts. You will ideally need an image file on floppy disk for Task 11.7.

Information: Clip art

Clip art can be used to add interest to a document but should only be used in an appropriate situation. For example, it might be used in an advertisement or notice for the staff noticeboard, but not in a business letter, although it might form part of a logo. Clip art can be moved, resized and copied. Word uses a clip art organizer arranged in categories which you can select from, or you can search by using a descriptive keyword. Clip art can also be found on disk, CD and on the Internet

For this section you will use the **Drawing toolbar**. To display this, select **Toolbars** from the **View** menu and **Drawing** from the side menu. There are many tools available to you and though not all are necessary for Level 2, you may like to experiment with them later.

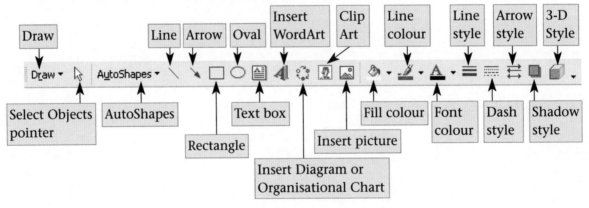

Figure 11.1 Drawing toolbar

Before you start, create a new folder called **WP2 Section 11**. Ensure you are working in Print Layout View.

Task 11.1 — Insert clip art, resize and move

Method

1   Open a new document and click on **Insert Clip Art** 🖼 on the Drawing toolbar. The Insert Clip Art Task pane appears (Figure 11.2).

> **Hint:** You can also select **Picture** from the **Insert** menu, and then **ClipArt** from the side menu.

2   In the **Search text:** box, key in **barn** and click on **Search**. Several pictures should appear, although yours may be different to those shown in Figure 11.3

Figure 11.2 Insert Clip Art Task pane

> **Hint:** If a search word gives no results, try another similar word, e.g. farm.

Figure 11.3 Search results

3   Click on a picture to select it – it then appears on the page.
4   To search for another picture, click on **Modify** and key in **car** as the search text. Click on **Search**. (Ensure the first picture is not selected or the new one will replace it.)
5   Depending on the pictures selected, their sizes will always differ. To resize the 'barn' picture, first ensure it is selected by clicking on it – 'handles' should appear on the sides and in each corner (Figure 11.4). Position the pointer over a corner handle until a double-headed arrow appears, then drag inwards to make it smaller, outwards to make it bigger.

> **Hint:** Always use a corner handle to resize. This keeps the image in proportion.

> **Note:** At this stage the image cannot be moved freely on the page as it is embedded in the text line (in line with text) and will only move along with any text. Text wrap needs to be applied to make it a floating object that can move independently of the text line.

Figure 11.4 Resize clip art

6 If not already selected, click on the image. The Picture toolbar should appear (Figure 11.5). If not, select **Toolbars** from the **View** menu and then select **Picture**.

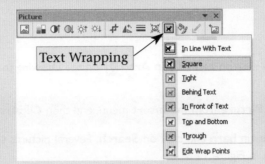

Figure 11.5 Picture toolbar

7 Click on the **Text Wrapping** button and select **Square**. Notice how the handles change, although they can still be used for resizing.

> **Note: Square** wrapping causes text to wrap around the image in a square shape.
> **Top and Bottom** wrapping causes it to stop above the picture and carry on below it.
> **Behind Text** removes text wrapping and places the object on a floating layer which would appear behind any text – suitable for display work, such as advertisements, as the text position is not affected by the picture. There are other options.

8 Position the pointer over the image – it changes to a four-headed arrow. Hold down the left mouse button and drag the image to a new position in the top middle of the page.

9 Save the document as **Graphics** into the **WP2 Section 11** folder.

These methods of moving and resizing can be used for any object.

Task 11.2   Use the Clip Organizer

The Clip Organizer holds clip art images stored in categories.

Method

1 If the Clip Art Task pane is not open, click on the **Insert Clip Art** button 🖼 on the drawing toolbar to open it and click on Clip Organizer 🖼 Clip Organizer... at the bottom of the Task pane.

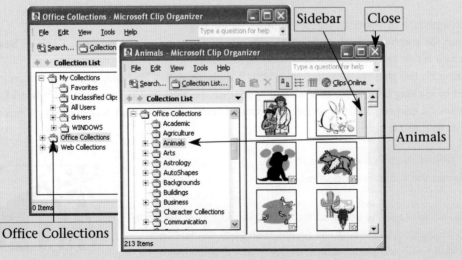

Figure 11.6 Clip Organizer

2   Double click on **Office Collections** (Figure 11.6). Click on the **Animals** folder and select a picture.

3   Click on the side bar on the right of the picture and select **Copy**.

4   Close the Clip Organizer by clicking on the red **Close** icon .

5   Click on the **Paste** button on the Formatting toolbar and the picture should appear. Apply **Square** text wrapping, resize and move the picture.

6   Try this several times using different categories e.g. People, Leisure, Nature.

7   Save the document.

Task 11.3	Adjust picture size to a specific height

The following method can be used for any object.

Method

I   Click on the barn picture to select it.

2   Choose **Picture** from the **Format** menu.

3   Select the **Size** tab (Figure 11.7).

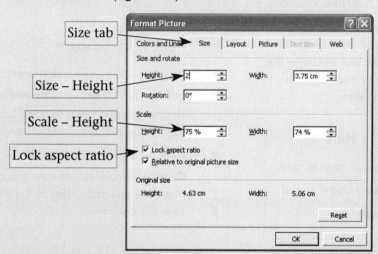

Figure 11.7 Resize to a specific height

4   Ensure **Lock aspect ratio** is checked (check box should be ticked). This ensures the image remains in proportion and is not distorted.

5   In the **Size – Height** box, key in a height of **2 cm**.

6   Click **OK**. The width will change in proportion.

7   Try this on other clipart images.

8   Delete all images except the barn picture.

9   Save the document.

Hint:

You do not need to key in cm, just the figure.

Note that you can also resize a picture by changing the scale by a percentage.

Task 11.4 — Add WordArt and group it with a picture to form a logo

Grouping objects together makes them easier to manipulate, as you only have to handle one object rather than several. This method can be used for any group of objects. Once objects are grouped together, you can also **ungroup** them if you should want to edit them in some way.

Method

1. Insert WordArt using the text **Barn Crafts**.
2. Resize the WordArt and position it below the picture as in Figure 11.8.

Figure 11.8 Select objects

3. To group the picture and WordArt together, click on the **Select Objects** pointer on the Drawing toolbar and position it at point 1 in Figure 11.8. Drag across and down to point 2. When the mouse button is released, handles appear on any objects enclosed in that space.
4. Click on the **Draw** button Draw ▾ on the Drawing toolbar and select **Group**. The objects are now grouped together.
5. Move the grouped object to the middle of the page.
6. Save the document.

Task 11.5 — Insert graphical shapes, fill and adjust size to specific measurements

Method

1. Select the **Rectangle** tool from the Drawing toolbar. The mouse pointer changes to a cross.
2. Hold down the left mouse button and drag to draw a small rectangle.
3. With the rectangle still selected (i.e. handles appear on the sides and corners), click on the down arrow alongside the **Fill Color** button on the Drawing toolbar and select a dark colour.
4. Resize the shape to a specific size by choosing **AutoShape** from the **Format** menu, and selecting the **Size** tab (as in Figure 11.7). Do *not* lock aspect ratio this time, as you do not want to keep it in proportion. Key in a height of **6 cm** and a width of **8 cm**. (This is quite large but will be resized in the next task.) Click **OK**.

Hint:

Lock aspect ratio keeps the shape in its original proportion. By *not* locking it, you can change the proportion of the height to the width.

Hint:

Fill Color 🪣 ▾ can be used on any shape and also on WordArt.

Hint:

The size of any object can be changed using the method in step 6.

5 Select the **Oval** ⬭ tool and draw an oval shape below the rectangle. The size does not matter. Use **Fill Color** 🪣 ▾ to fill it with a pale colour.

6 Select the oval. Choose **AutoShape** from the **Format** menu, and select the **Size** tab. Key in a height of **2.3 cm** and a width of **6 cm**. Do *not* lock aspect ratio.

7 Select the **WordArt** ◢ tool and the style as shown in Figure 11.9 on the next page.

 Key in the text **Barn Crafts**. Click **OK**.

8 Select the WordArt and use **Fill Color** 🪣 ▾ to colour it.

9 Resize using **WordArt** from the **Format** menu to a height of **1.2 cm** and a width of **3.1 cm**.

10 Save.

Task 11.6   Adjust the scale of an object

Using Scale options to resize an object allows you to use a percentage figure of the original size. This same method can be used for any object.

Method

1 Select the rectangle shape drawn above.
2 Using **AutoShape** from the **Format** menu and the **Size** tab, ensure that **Lock Aspect Ratio** is selected to keep the shape in its current proportion. Key in **50%** in the **Scale – Height** box and press **OK**.
3 Save.

Information: Working with layers

When you are working with several objects you may be required to position them one on top of another. By selecting an object you can adjust its position in the 'pile'. You are first aiming for a logo arranged as seen in Figure 11.9 but will experiment with the different options below to see how they work.

- **Bring to Front** brings the selected object to the front (or top of the pile).
- **Send to Back** sends the selected object to the back (or bottom of the pile).
- **Bring Forward** brings the object forward by one layer.
- **Send Backward** sends the object backward by one layer.
- **Bring in Front of Text** brings the object in front of any text so the text is obscured (hidden).
- **Send Behind Text** puts the object behind any text so the object can be seen in the background.

Task 11.7   Change layer order

Method

1   Move the oval shape on top of the rectangle.
2   Move the WordArt on top of the oval.
3   Now change the order of the layers by selecting the rectangle, click on the

Draw 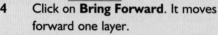 button and choose **Order**.
4   Click on **Bring Forward**. It moves forward one layer.
5   Select the oval, click on the **Draw** button and choose **Order**.
6   Click on **Bring to Front**.

Figure 11.9 Layers

Experiment with all options to see how they work. End up with the objects displayed as in Figure 11.9.

7   Now group together, as you did in Task 11.4.
8   Save the document.

Things to do

1   Draw a small rectangle shape and copy and paste it four times, placing the copies side by side and spaced across the page. Select the first shape, click on the drop down arrow alongside the **Fill Color** button 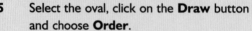 and select **Fill Effects**. Click on the **Pattern** tab and choose a pattern fill. Choose a different pattern fill for each shape. Save as **Things to Do** into **WP2 Section 11** folder.

2   On the same page, select the Line tool ╲ and press and drag to draw a line. (Hold down the Shift key to draw a perfect straight line.) Drag a handle to lengthen or shorten it. Drag on the line itself to move it. (It will only move when ✛ is visible.) Click on Line style ▤ to change the line thickness and then try Dash style ▤ . Now draw lines connecting the first rectangle drawn in step 1 above to the next one, and repeat for each. If a line overlaps a shape, send it back a layer. Change all the lines to different dashed styles. Save, print and close.

3   Open a new file. AutoShapes AutoShapes ▾ on the Drawing toolbar has several categories of shapes with which you can experiment. Try creating more examples of possible logos for Barn Crafts using different shapes from the categories **Basic Shapes** and **Stars and Banners**, as well as WordArt. Group each finished logo. Save as **Logos** into **WP2 Section 11** folder and print.

4   Using the same file, now try creating more logos using clip art, as well as shapes and WordArt.

Information: Photographic images and text wrapping

A photographic image file might be created by scanning a photograph and saving it, or by taking a picture with a digital camera that is then saved to disk. These images can be inserted into a Word file and **text wrapping** applied.

You will need an image on floppy disk for this task – ask your tutor.

Task 11.8 — Insert a photographic image and apply text wrapping

Method

1 Open the document **Conservatory Use** from **My Documents** (created in Section 3) and save it as **Conservatory with picture** into the **WP2 Section 11** folder. Position the cursor in the space between the first paragraph and the second heading.

2 Click on insert picture 🖼 on the Drawing toolbar.

3 Click on the down arrow alongside the **Look in:** box (Figure 11.10), and select **3½ Floppy (A:).** Select the picture required (you may see a list of pictures) and click on **Insert.** The picture appears, and, depending on its size, some of the text below it may have moved onto a second page.

> **Hint:**
> You can also select **Picture** from the **Insert** menu, and **From File** from the side menu.

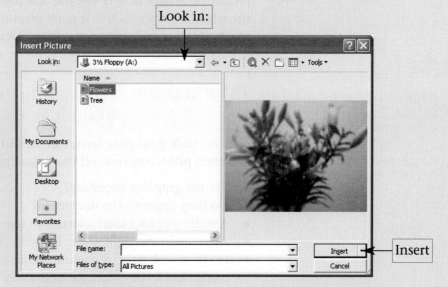

Figure 11.10 Insert picture

> **Hint:**
> Using a corner handle ensures that the picture stays in proportion.

4 The picture is **inline** – i.e. it is embedded in the text. Centre it using the text centre button ≡

5 Click on it to select it and drag a *corner* handle towards the middle of the picture to make it smaller. Ensure all the text is displayed on one page.

6   Ensure the picture is still selected. The Picture toolbar (Figure 11.5) should have appeared – if not select **Toolbars** from the **View** menu, and **Picture** from the side menu. To change the picture to a **floating** picture, click on the **Text Wrapping** button ⊞ and select **Square**. The text will now be shaped around the picture and the handles will have changed appearance.

7   Ensuring the picture is still selected, hold the left mouse button down and drag the picture across to the middle of the page. The text should now wrap all around the picture.

8   With the picture selected, click on the **Text Wrapping** button ⊞ and select **Top and Bottom**. The text should appear above and below the picture. Try other text wrap options ending up with **Square**.

9   With **Square** text wrap applied, move the picture to the right-hand side of the page alongside the first paragraph.

10 Save the file, print and close.

Information: Positioning images and other objects

It is important to place images and other objects so that the appearance of a document is improved. Images should add something to the document, not make it difficult for the reader. For example, if you move the picture to the middle of the page with square text wrapping, it makes it hard to read. This is because you read the text to the left of the picture and then your eyes have to jump across it and find the right line on the other side. This makes it easy to lose your place and then you lose the thread of the text. A good position for a picture on a page of text like the one used above, is anywhere around the edge. A corner is often a good position. If text wrap is applied top and bottom, then it is acceptable to place it in the middle of the page.

Information: Checking layout when using graphics

Always check your page layout when using graphics. Print preview first and then print. Ask yourself the following questions?

- Are the graphics necessary?
- Do they improve the document?
- Are the graphics used relevant to the document?
- Are they in the right place, i.e. with the text that relates to them?
- Do they look right? Sometimes adjusting the position or size a little can make all the difference to the way the text wraps around them.

Information: Inserting a chart

A chart is a way of displaying numbers in a pictorial way, making it easier to understand at a glance. Charts can be created within Word or copied and pasted from Excel (or even linked to), Word's companion spreadsheet program. This task assumes that Microsoft Graph Chart has been installed as part of the Office suite.

Task 11.9　Insert a chart

In this task you will create a memo and insert a chart displaying test results.

Method

I　Select **New** from the **File** menu, and choose the **Simple A4 memo** template you created in an earlier section.

2　Fill in the following information:

To:　**Kelly Wexford**

From:　**Your name**

Date:　**Today's date**

Subject: **Candidate Results**

3　Below this, key in:

Following our talk yesterday, the chart below shows the success of our candidates at the end of term. As you can see, the success rate is excellent, with no Fails and a high proportion of candidates gaining Credits and Distinctions.

4　Press **Enter** twice.

5　Click on the **Insert** menu and choose **Object** (Figure 11.11).

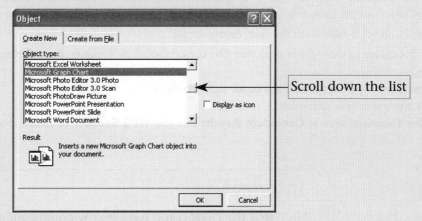

Figure 11.11 Insert object

6　Scroll down the list and select **Microsoft Graph Chart**. A sample chart appears, with a datasheet (Figure 11.12). The datasheet is where you key in the figures from which the chart will be created. It looks a little like a Word table, with cells arranged in columns and rows.

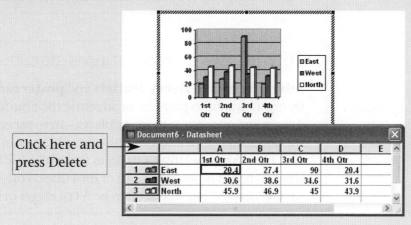

Figure 11.12 Create a chart

7 Click in the top left grey box (see above) to highlight the entire sheet and press **Delete** to delete the data.

8 Key in the new data as seen in Figure 11.13. Move across from one cell to another with the Tab key. If necessary widen the first column by positioning the pointer over the column boundary and when the four-headed **Move** arrow appears ✛, drag a little to the right.

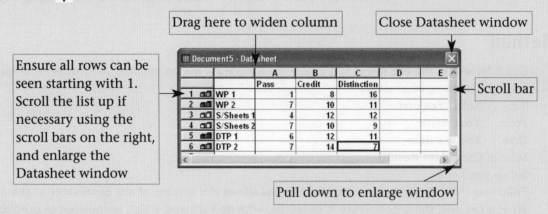

Drag here to widen column

Close Datasheet window

Ensure all rows can be seen starting with 1. Scroll the list up if necessary using the scroll bars on the right, and enlarge the Datasheet window

Scroll bar

Pull down to enlarge window

Figure 11.13 Enter data

9 Check the data carefully and then click on ☒ to close the Datasheet window. The chart remains.

10 Click on the chart and drag the right-hand side handle to enlarge the chart and to show all category labels at the bottom (Credit was probably hidden). Now click outside the chart area to return to text editing mode.

11 As the chart object is inline with the text, centre it ☰

12 Position the cursor to the right of the chart (the cursor should be flashing), press **Enter** twice and key in the following:

Please pass on my congratulations to all staff involved.

13 Align the last line of text to the left.

14 Check the document, save as **Candidate Results** into the **WP2 Section 11** folder, print and close.

Information

Note that the chart could have text wrapping applied to make it a floating object if required, but charts are quite likely to be inserted and remain as part of the text.

To edit the chart figures, double click on the chart and the Datasheet window reopens. Try it now and then close it again.

Information: Promotional documents

Advertisements, **flyers**, **leaflets** and **posters** are all documents used by organisations to promote or advertise their business or services. Advertisements appear in many places – newspapers, magazines, shop windows, billboards and giant hoardings! They can be just about any size. Flyers are generally A4 or A5 in size whilst leaflets are usually A4 in size and might be folded in half or into three. Posters are likely to be no smaller than A4 but would often be A3 or bigger in size.

Task 11.10 — Change character spacing

Method

1. Open a new document and key in your full name.
2. Copy and paste this four times and arrange one below the other.
3. Highlight the second line and select **Font** from the **Format** menu. Click on the **Character Spacing** tab (Figure 11.14).

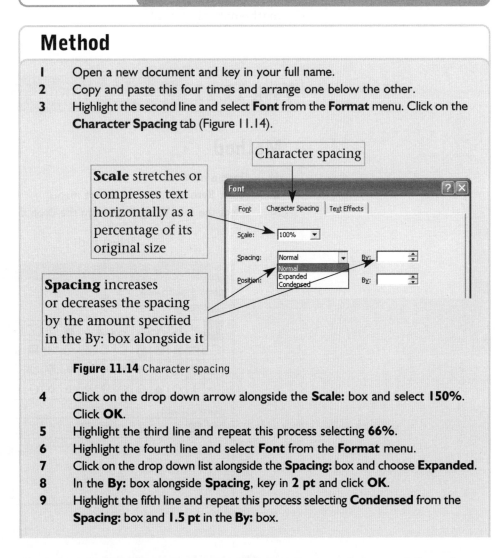

Scale stretches or compresses text horizontally as a percentage of its original size

Spacing increases or decreases the spacing by the amount specified in the By: box alongside it

Figure 11.14 Character spacing

4. Click on the drop down arrow alongside the **Scale:** box and select **150%**. Click **OK**.
5. Highlight the third line and repeat this process selecting **66%**.
6. Highlight the fourth line and select **Font** from the **Format** menu.
7. Click on the drop down list alongside the **Spacing:** box and choose **Expanded**.
8. In the **By:** box alongside **Spacing**, key in **2 pt** and click **OK**.
9. Highlight the fifth line and repeat this process selecting **Condensed** from the **Spacing:** box and **1.5 pt** in the **By:** box.

Experiment with this feature using different fonts and sizes and then close the file without saving.

Information: Symbols

Symbols are small graphical images that are part of a font's character set. Different fonts have different symbols. The following are examples of the Times New Roman and Wingdings font symbols.

Times New Roman   é ê â ç ½ ©
Wingdings   ☎ ✂ ⊠ ⊠ ✓ ▥

As they are in fact text characters, they can be made bigger or smaller in the same way as ordinary text – i.e. by highlighting and selecting a font size. This is also how you can insert foreign accents and mathematical symbols.

Task 11.11   Insert symbols

Method

1   Open a new file.
2   Select **Symbol** from the **Insert** menu.
3   Select the font **Wingdings** from the drop down list (Figure 11.15).

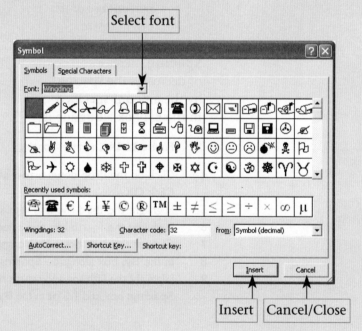

Figure 11.15 Insert symbols

4   Click on a symbol to select.
5   Click on **Insert**.
6   Repeat to insert several different symbols.
7   **Close** the Symbol dialogue box.
8   Change the size of the symbols by highlighting and selecting a font size.
9   Repeat the task trying different fonts.
10 Close the file without saving.

Information: Planning and preparing documents

When asked to produce a document you will often be given information from which to prepare it. This might consist of text, numerical information or images supplied on disk, copied from other files or supplied on paper. You should always check you have everything you need before you start.

Time spent drawing a rough sketch of the document layout may help you to think about what you need to do and could save you time in the end because it may avoid mistakes. You may be asked to draw a sketch in your test. A sketch for the next task (Practise your skills 11.1) is shown below.

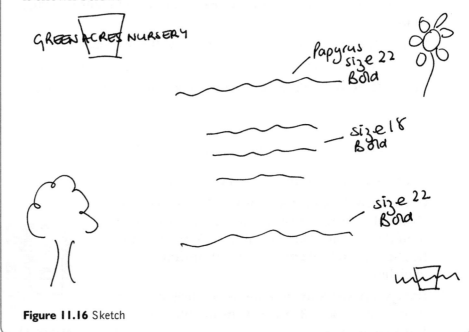

Figure 11.16 Sketch

→ Practise your skills 11.1

Produce a flyer

1 Open a new **A5 landscape** document with margins all round of **2 cm**.
2 Create the logo in Figure 11.17. The shape should be size **3 cm** by **3 cm** and filled with a light green colour.
3 Create the text using WordArt and fill with a dark colour.
4 Group the two objects together and move to the top left corner of the page.
5 Apply text wrap in the **Top and Bottom** style.
6 Key in the following:

    For all your gardening needs
    Monday–Friday 8 am–6 pm
    Saturday 8 am–6 pm
    Sunday 9 am–5 pm
    Langley Road, Bixford

Figure 11.17 Greentops logo

7 Centre the text and format to a font of your choice, bold and a suitable size.

8 Change the scale of character spacing of the first line to **150%**.

9 Copy the logo and reduce it to **50%** of its size, keeping aspect ratio.

10 Apply text wrap in the **Behind text** style and move the copied logo to the bottom right corner.

11 Insert a clip art image searching on the word **flower**. Apply **Behind text** style text wrapping and move it to the top right corner. Adjust the size to suit.

12 Insert a clip art image searching on the word **tree**. Apply **Behind text** style text wrapping and move it to the bottom left corner. Adjust the size to suit.

13 Check your layout still fits onto one page and use the spellcheck adding Bixford to the dictionary.

14 Save as **Greentops Flyer** into the **WP2 Skills Practice** folder and print.

15 Change the scale of all the text character spacing to **80%**.

16 Change the page setup to **A4 portrait** with top and bottom margins of **4 cm**, left and right set at **3 cm**.

17 Change the line spacing to **1.5** and increase the text size.

18 Increase the size of the clip art images and the *smaller* logo and adjust the layout to suit.

19 Save as **Greentops Flyer 2** into the same folder, print and close.

→ Practise your skills 11.2

1 Draw a sketch of this document before you start.

2 Open a new document and create a logo as seen in Figure 11.18. Use AutoShapes to draw a **Wave** shape from the Stars and Banners category. Resize this to a height of **2 cm** by **6 cm** and fill with **indigo** (dark blue).

3 Draw a **5-point Star** from the same category. Resize this shape to **3 cm** by **3 cm** and fill with **light turquoise**.

Figure 11.18 Boxford logo

4 Use WordArt to create the text and assemble the logo as shown, using Order options from Draw Draw ▾ if necessary to change the layer order.

5 Group the objects together and position in the top right corner. Apply **Top and Bottom** text wrapping so the text will start below it.

6 Key in the following text:

Boxford Conservatories coming to your area soon

We are a family business established in 1986

- **Great prices**
- **A variety of styles and finishes**
- **Delivery on time**
- **Experienced craftsmen fitters**
- **Satisfaction guaranteed or your money back**

If you are thinking of installing a conservatory in the near future call us now to see what we can do for you. You will be amazed at our prices and the choice of styles – there is sure to be something to fit your budget.

Call now on 01997 255643

7   Change the paper size to **20 cm** by **20 cm** and the margins to **2 cm** all round.

8   Insert a clip art image, apply **Square** text wrapping and position it on the left alongside the paragraph beginning **If you are thinking . . .** .

9   Choose appropriate fonts and size to display the text.

10   Centre the first and last lines.

11   **Expand** the character spacing of the last line by **2 pt**.

12   Proofread your work and check the layout – adjust the position or size of the image slightly if it will improve presentation.

13   Spellcheck, adding any names to the dictionary, and print preview.

14   Save as **Boxford Conservatories** into the **WP2 Skills Practice** folder, print and close.

15   Does your printout look like your sketch?

→ Practise your skills 11.3

Key in the following, using the font as indicated, for the symbols and accents.

1   Telephone us on ☎ 765434.   (Wingdings)

2   Le deuxième étage.   (Times New Roman)

3   ✉ e-mail us now!   (Wingdings)

4    $\frac{1}{4} + \frac{1}{2} = \frac{3}{4}$ (Times New Roman)

5   © Heinemann 2004   (Times New Roman)

→ Check your knowledge

1   When working with graphic objects, what does **lock aspect ratio** mean?

2   What is the difference between an **inline** and a **floating** graphic?

3   With **Square text wrapping** applied, where is a good position for an image and why?

4   What things should you consider when placing graphics on the page?

5   What is the purpose of grouping and ungrouping objects?

6   What is the purpose of a chart?

Consolidation 3

Here you will create a letter template with styles and insert a chart.

1 Open a new document and set the page up as **A4** with margins of **3 cm** all round.

2 Copy and paste the large logo from **Greentops Flyer** in **WP2 Section 11** folder, placing it on the top right of the page.

3 Apply **Square** text wrapping to the logo (as the address will appear alongside).

4 Modify the **Normal** style to be **Arial** size **11**.

5 Key in the address and telephone number in the top left corner of the page:

Langley Road

Bixford

BX7 9RD

Tel: 019966 654777

6 Create a new style called **Heading** with **Arial** font, size **12**, **bold** with the style for the **following paragraph** to be **Normal**.

7 Apply this style to the address and telephone number.

8 Press **Enter** twice below the telephone number.

9 Use the underscore key to create a line halfway across the page. Press **Enter** and Word will insert a bold line across the page. Ensure the logo is fully above the line.

10 Below the line, press **Enter** twice and insert the date to update automatically.

11 Save the file as a document template with the name **Greentops letter**.

12 Close the template and open a copy of it using **New** from the **File** menu.

13 Key in the following:

Mr A Shafi

GroFasta Products

Anytown

Anywhere

AN1 5WH

Dear Mr Shafi

GroFasta Fertilizer

It is now three months since we agreed to stock your new product GroFasta at special discount rates and, as agreed, we have carried out checks to see how your product has sold over the last six weeks. This is best illustrated by the chart below.

Sales of GroFasta showing sales in hundreds

14 Insert a chart using the following data (Figure 11.19):

C:\My Documents\Consolidat... - Datasheet			A	B	C	D	E	F	
			Week 1	Week 2	Week 3	Week 4	Week 5	Week 6	
1		GroFasta	1	2	5	6	6	5	
2		Competitor	2	3	2	2	1	1	
3									
4									

Figure 11.19 GroFasta chart

15 Centre the chart and use a side handle to make it wider so all labels are displayed.

16 Key in the following below the chart.

As you can see sales increased significantly following your national advertising campaign, whilst your main competitor's went down. I enclose a further breakdown of the daily figures. I hope this information will be useful to you and I look forward to negotiating continued discount rates with you.

Yours sincerely

Your name
Manager

Enc

17 Apply the style **Heading** that you created to the main heading and to the graph heading.
18 Check your work for layout and errors. Add any proper names to the spellcheck dictionary.
19 Save as **GroFasta letter** into the **Consolidation** folder and print.
20 Save a copy of the file into the **Backup** folder on floppy disk and close.

Document editing and formatting

You will learn to

- Insert files
- Create sections
- Create columns
- Use Find and Replace

You have already copied and pasted text between files. In this section you will use another method of combining files by inserting one file inside another. You will also find out how to divide documents into sections and create columns. The Find and Replace feature, previously covered at Level 1, is looked at again in this section.

Create a folder called **WP2 Section 12**.

Information: Inserting a file

In Section 2 you copied and pasted text between files. Another way of combining files is to insert one file inside another.

Task 12.1   Insert a file

In this task you will insert two files into a new file. Both of these files were created at the end of Section 7 and saved in the **WP2 Skills Practice** folder.

Method

1	Open a new document, A4 portrait with default margins.
2	Key in the following: **INFORMATION FOR RECEPTION STAFF** **Listed below are the evening courses for this term. Please refer to this list for any telephone or personal enquiries.**
3	Embolden the heading, increase its size to **20** and the paragraph text to size 14.
4	Press return twice below the paragraph and select **File** from the **Insert** menu (Figure 12.1).
5	Select the **WP2 Skills Practice** folder and click on **Open**.
6	Select the **Evening Courses** file and click on **Insert** (Figure 12.2). The file is inserted.

Hint:

You can also double click on the folder name to open it and then on the filename to insert it.

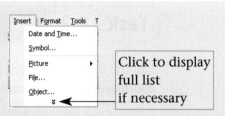

Figure 12.1 Insert file

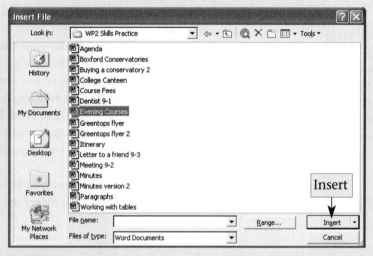

Figure 12.2 Select file

7 Press **Enter** twice and select **File** from the **Insert** menu again.
8 Select the **Course Fees** file and click on **Insert** as before. The file is inserted.
9 Check that the text formatting is consistent, e.g. similar headings are the same size, body text is the same size.
10 Add your name and the date to the footer.
11 Save the file as **Reception information** into the **WP2 Section 12** folder, print and close.

Hint:

You should always check the formatting of combined files as they may be different.

Information: Sections

Files you have created so far have consisted of one continuous section. It is possible to divide a document into sections and then to format each section differently, for example by dividing it into columns, giving the sections different headers or footers or even applying different orientation (landscape or portrait). Open a new blank document and look in the status bar in the bottom left corner of the window to see the section number (Figure 12.3).

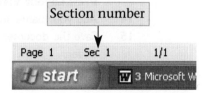

Figure 12.3 Section

Task 12.2 — Insert a continuous section break

Use the blank document just opened. You are now going to enter a command that will generate some text on the page for you to work with.

Hint:

This is a useful trick for placing text onto the page to experiment with. Each sentence uses all the letters of the alphabet.

Method

1   Key in the heading **Working with Sections and Columns** and press **Enter** twice.
2   Key in **=rand(1,20)** and press **Enter** twice.
3   Key in the heading **Subheading** and press **Enter** twice.
4   Key in **=rand(1,20)** again and press **Enter** twice.
5   Key in the heading **Subheading** and press **Enter** twice.
6   Key in **=rand(1,20)** again. Press **Enter**. You should have a main heading, two subheadings and three paragraphs of text.
7   Apply **Heading style 1** to the main heading and **Heading style 3** to the two subheadings.
8   Position the cursor directly in front of and to the left of the first paragraph. Select **Break** from the **Insert** menu (Figure 12.4).

A section break will usually be either **Next page**, which starts a new section on a new page, or **Continuous**, which continues on the current page

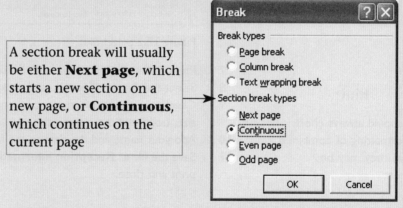

Figure 12.4 Insert a break

9   Click on **Continuous** and click **OK**. Look at the status bar and note that the cursor is now in Section 2.
10   Position the cursor directly in front of and to the left of the first subheading. Select **Break** from the **Insert** menu.
11   Click on **Continuous** and click **OK**. Look at the status bar and note that the cursor is now in Section 3.
12   Repeat this process in front of the second paragraph, the second subheading and the last paragraph. You should end up with six sections.
13   Switch to **Normal View** and you can see the section breaks. Switch back to **Print Layout View**.
14   Add your name and the date to the footer.
15   Save the document as **Sections and Columns** into the **WP2 Section 12** folder.

Information: Columns

Word documents can be arranged in newspaper style columns. The use of sections means that different sections can have a different number of columns. Work in **Print Layout View** to display columns side by side. **Normal View** displays all text in only a single column even when there is more than one.

Task 12.3　Create columns

Method

I　Click inside the first paragraph – the status bar should read Sec 2. Click on the **Columns** button ▤ and drag across to highlight and select the number of columns required – in this case **2** (Figure 12.5). The text should appear in columns.

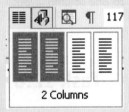

Figure 12.5 Select columns

2　Click inside the last paragraph (Section 6) and repeat this action.

3　Print preview the page and print.

Task 12.4　Change the column layout

Method

I　Position the cursor inside the first paragraph (Section 2). Click on the **Columns** button ▤ and drag across to highlight one column.

2　Position the cursor inside the second paragraph (Section 4). Click on the **Columns** button ▤ and drag across to highlight two columns.

3　Position the cursor inside the third paragraph (Section 6). Click on the **Columns** button ▤ and drag across to highlight three columns.

4　Print preview and print.

Columns can also be formatted by selecting **Columns** from the **Format** menu. This gives options for choosing column widths and also for putting a line between columns. This can look effective. Try these now, remembering to click into the appropriate section first.

You should end up with the first paragraph in three columns, the second paragraph in two columns and the third in one column.

Task 12.5 — Delete section breaks

Method

1   Switch to **Normal View** which shows the type and position of the break – in this case **Continuous** as a double dotted line (Figure 12.6).

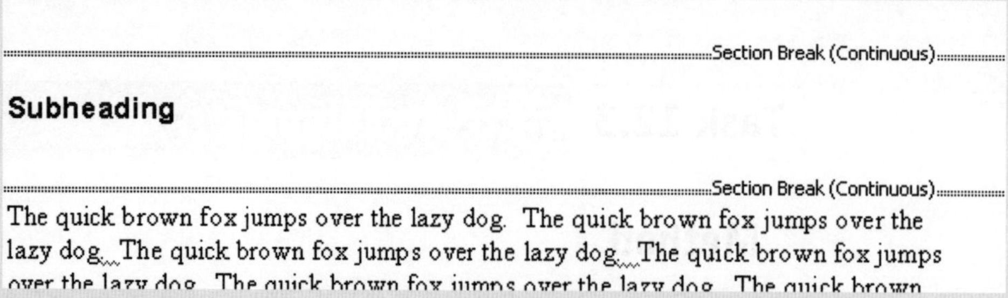

··Section Break (Continuous)·············

Subheading

··Section Break (Continuous)·············

The quick brown fox jumps over the lazy dog. The quick brown fox jumps over the lazy dog. The quick brown fox jumps over the lazy dog. The quick brown fox jumps over the lazy dog. The quick brown fox jumps over the lazy dog. The quick brown

---

Figure 12.6 Section breaks

2   Click on a dotted line and press **Delete**. Repeat to remove all of the breaks.
3   Change the document to one column layout.

Task 12.6 — Create sections and columns at the same time

This is a quick method of putting text into columns and creating sections at the same time.

Method

1   Highlight the first paragraph.
2   Click on the **Columns** button ▦ and drag across to highlight and select two columns. The text in that paragraph should appear in columns and the document should be in three sections.
3   Highlight the second paragraph.
4   Click on the **Columns** button ▦ and drag across to highlight and select three columns. The text in that paragraph should appear in columns and the document should be in five sections.
5   Highlight the last paragraph.
6   Click on the **Columns** button ▦ and drag across to highlight and select two columns. The text in that paragraph should appear in columns and the document should be in six sections.

> **Information:** Next page section breaks
>
> You have already created page breaks in Section 2. **Next page** section breaks start a new page but also create a new section at the same time. You can then, for example, change the orientation of the different sections. In this task you will end up with three pages, the first and last will be portrait and the middle one will be landscape. This might be useful if you have, for example, a wide table to display.

Task 12.7 — Insert next page section breaks

Method

1	Delete the section breaks and ensure the document is in a single column.
2	Position the cursor directly in front of and to the left of the first subheading. Select **Break** from the **Insert** menu.
3	Click on **Next page** to end up with two pages (and two sections).
4	Repeat in front of the second subheading to end up with three pages (and three sections).
5	Position the cursor on the second page (Section 2) and choose **Page Setup** from the **File** menu.
6	Click on the **Margins** tab and select **Landscape** orientation. Click **OK**.
7	**Print preview** the document showing all three pages.
8	Add the page number to the footer. **Print preview**, save, print and close.

Information: Column breaks

Sometimes you might be required to change where the text breaks to start a new column. This is when you use a **column break**. When you insert a column break, Word moves any text that follows to the top of the next column.

Task 12.8 — Insert column breaks

Method

1	Open a new document and change the page setup to landscape.
2	Key in the heading **Using Column Breaks** and press **Enter** twice.
3	Key in the subheading **First subheading** and press **Enter** twice.
4	Key in =**rand(1,15)** and press **Enter** twice.
5	Key in the subheading **Second subheading** and press **Enter** twice.
6	Key in =**rand(1,10)** and press **Enter** twice.
7	Key in the subheading **Third subheading** and press **Enter** twice.
8	Key in =**rand(1,5)** and press **Enter** once.
9	Position the cursor in front of and to the left of the first subheading and insert a **continuous** section break.
10	**Centre** the main heading and format it as **bold**, size 14.
11	Format the three subheadings as **bold**.
12	Position the cursor in Section 2 and format the text into three columns.
13	Position the cursor in front of and to the left of the second subheading and select **Break** from the **Insert** menu.
14	Select **Column break** (Figure 12.7) and click **OK**.
15	Position the cursor in front of and to the left of the third subheading and select **Break** from the **Insert** menu.
16	Select **Column break** and click **OK**. The second and third subheadings should appear at the top of the second and third columns.

17   Add your name to the footer on the left and the date on the right.

Figure 12.7 Column break

18   Save as **Using Column Breaks** into the **WP2 Section 12** folder, print and close.

Information: Find and replace

Sometimes you may wish to replace a word throughout a document with a different word, e.g. change *he* to *she*. As you learnt in Level 1, Word has a feature called **Find and Replace** that can look through a document to **Find** a word and **Replace** it each time it occurs.

Task 12.9   Use Find and Replace All

Replace All will find a word and replace every occurrence of that word throughout an entire document.

Method

1   Open a new document, key in **=rand(1,20)** and press **Enter**.
2   Select **Replace** from the **Edit** menu.
3   In the **Find what:** box, key in **quick** (Figure 12.8).

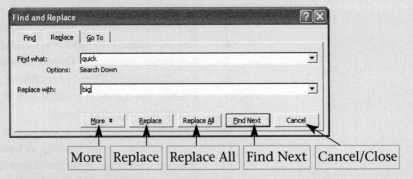

Figure 12.8 Find and Replace All

4   In the **Replace with:** box, key in **big**.
5   Click on **Replace All**. A message appears to say that 20 replacements have been made. Click **OK**.
6   Click on the **Close** button.
7   Repeat this process, finding **lazy** and replacing with **sleeping**.

Hint:

If Find and Replace does not work as expected, click on **Undo** and try again

Find Next allows you to choose whether or not to replace the search word, stopping each time the word is found. You can then choose to replace it or find the next one.

Method

1. Select **Replace** from the **Edit** menu.
2. Key in **dog** in the **Find what:** box and **cat** in the **Replace with:** box.
3. Click on **Find Next**. Word finds and highlights the word **dog**.
4. Click on **Replace**. The word is replaced and Word automatically highlights the next occurrence of the word. This gives you the chance to **Replace** again or to **Find Next** if you do not want to replace it.
5. Click on **Replace** and repeat until the message appears to say that Word has finished searching the document. Click **OK**.
6. Repeat this process finding **fox** and replacing with **dog**.
7. Close the Find and Replace dialogue box.
8. Save the file as **Search and Replace** into the **WP2 Section 12** folder, print and close.

Remember:

Upper case means capital letters, lower case means small letters.
Whole word is used when you want to look only for whole words that match the search word. It will not find words that form part of longer words. For example, the word <u>and</u> is found in s<u>and</u>, <u>And</u>rew, H<u>and</u>sworth and so on.

Information: Find and Replace – more options

Find and Replace has a number of further options, the most common of which are **Match case** and **Whole word**.

Match case is used to distinguish between upper and lower case letters. Only those words where the capital letters match those in the Find what: box are found.

Task 12.11 — Use Find and Replace – more options

Method

1. Open a new document and key in the following text.

   The Board of Directors of AT have recognised that changes must be made at Group Management Team level. Three years ago AT was a flourishing business in all respects and it is our wish that this should continue over the coming year.

   The review of AT's trading results will be detailed next week by Mark Cairns at the conference at the Sands Hotel in Handsworth.
   This year has been a difficult one for AT since so many of our activities depend upon the economic climate in other countries. AT's sales in the United States fell whilst those in Europe maintained a marked growth pattern. AT's future in the United States will be the subject of a Study to be announced at a later date.

An announcement on the new plant site for AT in the United Kingdom will be made at next month's Board Meeting, and this will allow further development of AT's interests in the home market.

2   Save the file into **WP2 Section 12** folder as **Find and Replace**.

Information

Notice the name of the company is <u>AT</u> but the letters <u>at</u> also occur elsewhere in the text, as the word <u>at</u>, in clim<u>at</u>e, St<u>at</u>es, p<u>at</u>tern and so on. The name <u>Mark</u> also appears as part of the words <u>mark</u>ed and <u>mark</u>et.

You will now see some of the unexpected results that can occur with Find and Replace.

3   Select **Replace** from the **Edit** menu. Key in **Mark** in the **Find what:** box and **Marc** in the **Replace with:** box. Click **Replace All**. A message tells you 3 replacements have been made. Click **OK** and **Close**. Whilst the name <u>Mark</u> has been replaced in paragraph two, so has <u>mark</u>ed and <u>mark</u>et in paragraphs three and four.

4   Click on **Undo** to undo the action.

5   Select **Replace** from the **Edit** menu. The same words will still be in the **Find what:** and **Replace with:** boxes.

6   Click on the **More** button for More options and select **Find whole words only** (Figure 12.9).

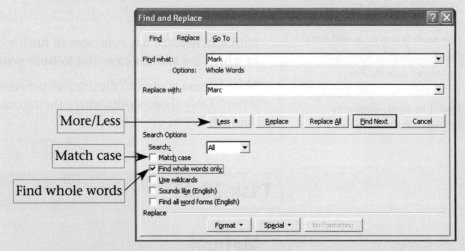

Figure 12.9 More/Less

7   Click **Replace All**. This time the word <u>Mark</u> is replaced only once – in the second paragraph. Click **OK** and **Close** Find and Replace.

Now you will see what can happen when **Match case** is not used when it should be.

8   Select **Replace** from the **Edit** menu. Key in **AT** in the **Find what:** box and **Ava Technics** in the **Replace with:** box. Click **Replace All**. A message tells you 13 replacements have been made. Click **OK** and **Close**. Look at the results. Because **Find whole words** is still checked on, it has replaced <u>AT</u> but also <u>at</u> where it occurred as a whole word, although not where it occurs in the middle of other words. The case of the original text has been followed.

9   Click on **Undo** to undo the action.

10   Select **Replace** from the **Edit** menu. The same words will still be in the **Find what:** and **Replace with:** boxes.

11 With **More** options still showing, click on **Match case** and then **Replace All**. A message tells you 8 replacements have been made. Click **OK** and **Close**. Look at the results. This time it has replaced as expected.

12 Add your name in the footer. Save the file, print and close.

→ Practise your skills 12.1

1 Open a new A4 document.

2 Key in the following text:

The Planning Stage

Before a project can begin, this is what should be considered:

- **What is required?**
- **When does it have to be completed?**
- **What resources are needed, e.g. materials, equipment, finance?**
- **What are the main tasks?**
- **Can some tasks be carried out at the same time or can they overlap?**
- **Which tasks have to be finished before others can begin?**
- **When does each separate task have to be completed?**
- **Who is responsible for what?**
- **Is the best use made of each team member's individual qualities, experience, knowledge and skills?**

REMEMBER – make sure everyone knows what is going on. A winning team works together.

3 Change the bullet style to check boxes.

4 Proofread and spellcheck. Save as **The Planning Stage** into the **WP2 Skills Practice** folder and close.

5 Open a new A4 portrait document and key in the heading **PROJECT TEAMS**. Press **Enter** twice.

6 Insert the file **Team Working** from **My Documents**.

7 Ensure there is one clear line space following the previous text and then insert the file **The Planning Stage** from the **WP2 Skills Practice** folder.

8 Embolden the main heading, centre it and enlarge it to size **14**.

9 Embolden the two subheadings.

10 Insert the cursor to the left in front of the subheading **Team Working** and insert a **continuous** section break.

11 Format Section 2 as two columns.

12 Insert the cursor to the left in front of the subheading **The Planning Stage** and insert a **column break**.

13 Insert a clip art image (search on the keyword **team or people**) and place it below the first paragraph with **Top and Bottom** text wrapping.

→

14 Insert a clip art image (search on the keyword **meeting**) and place it between the bulleted list and the last paragraph with **Top and Bottom** text wrapping.

15 Make any necessary adjustments to the size of the images.

16 Add your name on the left in the footer and insert the filename using Insert AutoText options on the right .

17 Save the file as **Project Teams** into the **WP2 Skills Practice** folder.

18 Print and close.

→ Practise your skills 12.2

1 Open the file **Find and Replace** from the **WP2 Section 12** folder. Carry out the following, checking each time to see if you have the desired results.

2 Replace **Ava Technics** with **AT**.

3 Replace **United States** with **USA**.

4 Replace **United Kingdom** with **UK**.

5 Replace **Marc** with **Mark**.

6 Replace **and** with **&**.

7 This is not good word processing practice, so change **&** back to **and**.

8 Check the file through carefully. Save, print and close.

→ Check your knowledge

1 What is a continuous section break?

2 What is a next page section break?

3 What is the quick way of creating columns and inserting a section break at the same time?

4 What happens to text that follows a column break?

5 What is Find and Replace?

6 What can you do to avoid replacing words that form part of longer words, e.g. <u>and</u> that occurs in <u>sand</u> and <u>Andrew</u>?

Mail merge

You will learn to

- Create standard documents
- Create data files
- Set up and carry out mail merge

This last section introduces mail merge. Think of all the letters that are sent out and addressed to you personally. Many of them are junk mailshots to try and make you buy something. Of course, someone does not sit typing out a letter to each person on the list. It is done by a process called mail merge – an efficient way of sending out the same letter to many people. The great advantage is that only one letter has to be produced. However, letters are not the only documents that can be merged.

Information: Mail merge

Mail merge is a process whereby a standard document, most commonly a letter, is merged with data from another file, such as a list of names and addresses, to produce many individual documents.

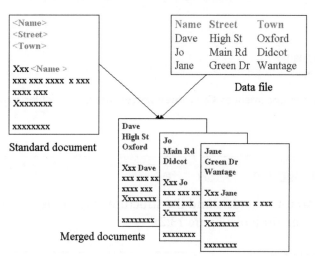

Figure 13.1 The mail merge process

In the example in Figure 13.1, a **data file** holds the list of names and addresses. The **standard document** has placeholders where the names and addresses will later appear. When the mail merge has been carried out, the content of the letter is the same every time, but the name and address will vary from one letter to the next.

Task 13.1 — Create a standard document – a letter

You are going to create a letter and send it to a list of customers. It is best to close down any open documents before you start.

Method

1 Open a new document and key in the following:

Today's date *[press Enter three times]*

Dear

This month we are celebrating our tenth anniversary and we want you to share in our celebration.

As a valued customer we are pleased to offer you a 10% discount on any goods ordered this month. One of our representatives will be contacting you shortly to give you more information on additional special offers that are also available.

Yours sincerely

Your name
Manager

2 Save the document as **Customer Letter** into a new folder called **WP2 Section 13** and leave it open.

Information: Data files

It is important to understand the structure of data files. Here is how the data file for a list of customers might look (Figure 13.2).

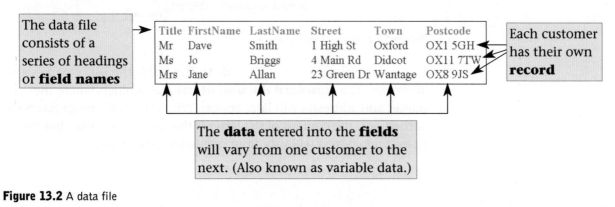

The data file consists of a series of headings or **field names**

Title	FirstName	LastName	Street	Town	Postcode
Mr	Dave	Smith	1 High St	Oxford	OX1 5GH
Ms	Jo	Briggs	4 Main Rd	Didcot	OX11 7TW
Mrs	Jane	Allan	23 Green Dr	Wantage	OX8 9JS

Each customer has their own **record**

The **data** entered into the **fields** will vary from one customer to the next. (Also known as variable data.)

Figure 13.2 A data file

Task 13.2 | Create a data file

Method

1   Open a new document.
2   From the **Table** menu, select **Insert** and from the side menu select **Table**.
3   Key in **6** for the number of columns and **6** for the number of rows.
4   Key in the field names in the first row and the data in the rows underneath, as seen below. It does not matter if the text wraps within a cell, although you can turn the page around to landscape if you wish.

Title	Firstname	Lastname	Street	Town	Postcode
Mr	Dave	Smith	1 High Street	Oxford	OX1 5GH
Ms	Jo	Briggs	4 Main Road	Didcot	OX11 7TW
Mrs	Jane	Allan	23 Green Drive	Wantage	OX8 9JS
Mr	Erik	Olsen	19 Manor Court	Oxford	OX1 7GG
Miss	Rhiannon	Lloyd	178 Porchester Street	Oxford	OX4 9JF

5   Check the data carefully and save the file as **Customer List** into the new **WP2 Section 13** folder. Print the data file and close it.

Task 13.3 | Set up the mail merge

Note: Make sure **Customer Letter** is the current open document and the data file is closed before going further.

Method

1   Select **Toolbars** from the **View** menu and then **Mail Merge**. (Some buttons will be greyed out at this point and therefore unavailable.)

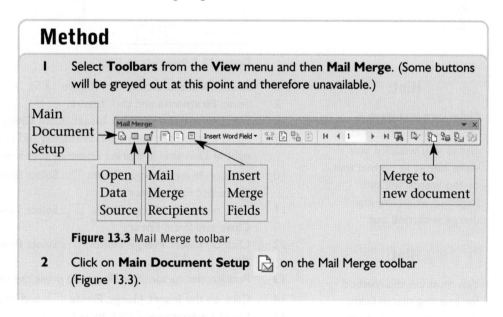

Figure 13.3 Mail Merge toolbar

2   Click on **Main Document Setup** on the Mail Merge toolbar (Figure 13.3).

3 Select **Letters** as the Main Document Type and click **OK** (Figure 13.4).

Figure 13.4 Main document type

4 Click on **Open Data Source** 🔳 . Locate the **Customer List** and click **Open**.
Note: The data source file is not actually opened but is linked to the letter.

5 Position the cursor in the space below the date. This is where the address fields will be placed. Click on **Insert Merge Fields** 📄 .

Merge fields act as placeholders for the data from the data source file.

Figure 13.5 Insert Merge Field

6 Select **Title** and click **Insert** (Figure 13.5).
7 Select **Firstname** and click **Insert**.
8 Select **Lastname** and click **Insert**. Click **Close**.
9 Insert a space between Title, Firstname and Lastname. Position cursor to the right of Lastname and press **Enter** to start a new line.
10 Click on **Insert Merge Fields** 📄 . Select **Street** and click **Insert**. Click **Close** and Press **Enter.**
11 Click on **Insert Merge Fields** 📄 . Select **Town** and click **Insert**. Click **Close** and Press **Enter.**
12 Click on **Insert Merge Fields** 📄 . Select **Postcode** and click **Insert**. Click **Close**.
13 Position the cursor after **Dear** and press the **spacebar** once.
14 Click on the **Insert Merge Fields** 📄 and select **Title**. Click **Insert**.
15 Select **Lastname** and click **Insert**.
16 Insert a space between Title and Lastname.

The inserted fields should look like the example in Figure 13.6. Notice how two fields are used twice. Note the spaces between the fields where they are needed.

«Title» «Firstname» «Lastname»
«Street»
«Town»
«Postcode»

Dear «Title» |«Lastname»

Figure 13.6 Inserted merge fields

17 Save the letter as **Discount Letter with merge fields** into the **WP2 Section 13** folder and print.

Task 13.4 Merge the data file with the document

You could choose to merge to the printer, but it is always a good idea to merge to a new document before printing to make sure the merge process has worked as expected. If you were merging a hundred letters you would waste a lot of paper if there was an error.

Method

1 Ensure the Mail Merge toolbar is still visible and click on **Merge to New Document** .

2 Ensure **All** records is selected (Figure 13.7) and click **OK**.

Figure 13.7 Merge to new document

3 The letters will appear in one new document, each letter separated by a section page break. Scroll through the letters to check the merge has been successful. You should have five letters, in five sections over five pages. If there is a problem, e.g. no space between parts of the name, close the merged letters to return to the original letter holding the merge fields and make any corrections. Then repeat from no. 1.

4 Save the letter as **Merged Discount Letter** into **WP2 Section 13** folder and print.

Task 13.5 Selecting recipients

When carrying out a mail merge, sometimes you may be required to produce letters using only selected records held within the data file. For example, you may need to send a letter to a particular person or only to those living in Oxford.

Method

Close the file **Merged Discount Letter,** saving if necessary. The **Discount Letter** showing the merge fields should be visible. If not, select it from the **Window** menu. Let us suppose that you need to produce a letter only for **Erik Olsen.**

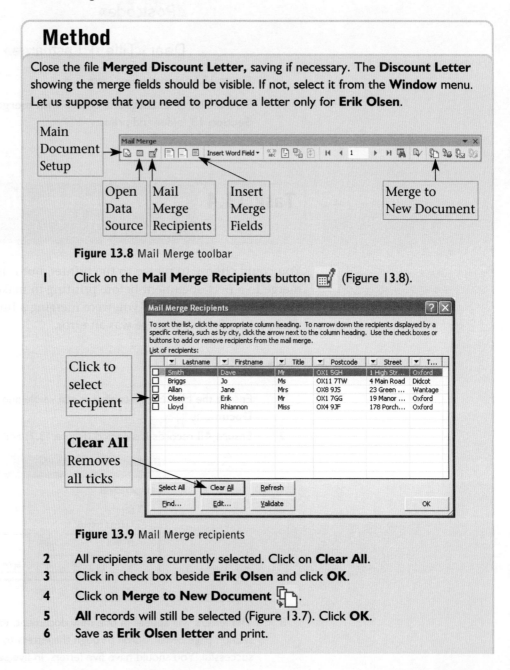

Figure 13.8 Mail Merge toolbar

I   Click on the **Mail Merge Recipients** button 🔲 (Figure 13.8).

Figure 13.9 Mail Merge recipients

2   All recipients are currently selected. Click on **Clear All**.
3   Click in check box beside **Erik Olsen** and click **OK**.
4   Click on **Merge to New Document** 🔲.
5   **All** records will still be selected (Figure 13.7). Click **OK**.
6   Save as **Erik Olsen letter** and print.

Task 13.6 Filter recipients

This time you will merge letters to only those living in Oxford. Close the Erik Olsen letter. The **Discount Letter** file showing the field codes should be visible.

Method

1   Click on the **Mail Merge Recipients** button 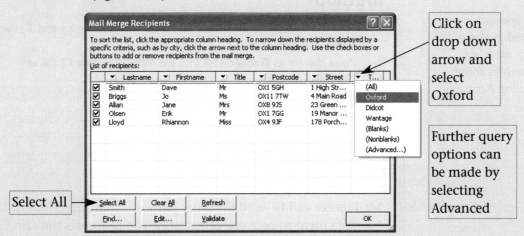 (Figure 13.8).

2   Click on **Select All** (Figure 13.10).

Figure 13.10 Filter recipients

3   Pick the field (column heading) on which you want to search – in this case **Town**. Click on the drop down arrow and select **Oxford**. Only the Oxford recipients should then be displayed. Click **OK**.

    Note: It is possible to search on more than one field.

4   Click on **Merge to New Document** 📑.

5   **All** records will still be selected (Figure 13.7). Click **OK**.

6   You should have three letters. Save as **Oxford customers** and print.

7   Close all documents.

Information: Planning data files

When planning data files you have to consider ways of dealing with the data you are working with. In the example below some of the addresses have a different number of lines.

Title	Initial	Lastname	Address1	Address2	Town	County	Postcode
Mr	P	Hesketh	24 The Moors		Poole	Dorset	BH23 5TW
Mrs	L	Rana	78 Castle View	Meadowside	Christchurch	Dorset	BH10 7KH
Mr and Mrs	G	Elliot	Albany House	129 Wanstead Road	Bournemouth	Dorset	BH11 7WZ
Ms	J	Connor	Flat 4	32 Holly Drive	Christchurch	Dorset	BH10 9KL
Mr and Mrs	I	Paulik	1 Cholwell Drive		Bournemouth	Dorset	BH11 2QS
Miss	L	Hamilton	9 Perivale View		Southampton	Hants	SO22 9FR

Notice how Address1 and Address2 cope with this. It is quite a common way of dealing with addresses. The important point to note is that the Town and County data is entered into the correct fields. This ensures the address is set out properly in the letters and makes it possible to query on those fields if required.

Task 13.7　Create a data file

Hint:

A data file does not have to be created in Word. It may already exist in a database, such as those produced using Access or Excel.

Method

1　Open a new document and insert a table of **8** columns and **7** rows.
2　Enter the data as above.
3　Save the file as **Garage List** into the **WP2 Section 13** folder.
4　Print the file and close it. You will use it later.

Information: Mail merge with other types of document

Mail merge can be used for other purposes apart from letters, for example memos, permits, certificates. The process is the same. In this task you will create a memo to send to staff who will be attending different training sessions.

Task 13.8　Mail merge a memo

Method

1　Select **New** from the **File** menu and select the **Simple A5 memo** template you set up for an earlier section.
2　Key in the following information. The asterisks (*) indicate where you will insert the merge fields later.

To:	*, * Department
From:	*Your name*
Date:	*Today's date*
Subject:	*Training Course

I confirm your place on the above course, which will be held on * starting promptly at * in the Training Room. If you are unable to attend, please let me know immediately.

3　Save the memo as **Course confirmation memo** into **WP2 Section 13** folder and print. Leave this file open.

4   Below is a sample of information from which you must set up the data file. Decide on the field names you need to use and draw on a piece of paper how you will set up the field names and how Dave Cooper's details will be entered. Check with the suggested answer at the end of this task and then set up a table with the required number of columns and enter the field names. Now enter the details shown below under the correct field name.

Dave Cooper	Bjorn Nilsson	Jean May	Pete Green
Sales	Personnel	Sales	Accounts
Advanced Word	Advanced Word	Intro to Access	Advanced Excel
12 June	12 June	27 June	23 June
9.30 am	9.30 am	2.30 pm	10 am

Ali London	Pam Clements	Bob Johns	Doug Richards
Marketing	Accounts	Marketing	Sales
Intro to Access	Advanced Excel	Advanced Excel	Advanced Word
27 June	23 June	23 June	12 June
2.30 pm	10 am	10 am	9.30 am

5   Save the data file as **Course List** into the **WP2 Section 13** folder and print.

6   Close the **Course List** and ensure **Course confirmation memo** is open.

7   Ensure the Mail Merge toolbar is visible (**View – Toolbars – Mail Merge**).

8   Click on **Main Document Setup** (Figure 13.3).

9   Select **Letters** as the Main Document Type and click **OK**.

10   Click on **Open Data Source**. Locate the **Course List** and click **Open**.

11   Insert the appropriate merge fields in place of the asterisks (*).

12   Merge to a new document. Check it and print. If you have A5 paper, load it into the printer, if not print on A4.

13   Save as **Merged course memos** into **WP2 Section 13** folder. Close all files.

Were the fields for your data file similar to these?

Name	Department	Course	Date	Time
Dave Cooper	Sales	Advanced Word	12 June	9.30 am

Information: Labels

Other documents that can be merged with data files are labels. These include mailing labels, name badges, disk and folder labels. To create these you would probably only use the contents of the fields and would not require any additional text. Labels are printed on sheets (often self-adhesive sheets). The number of labels on each sheet depends on the size of the label. In the work situation you must obviously check you have the right product to print on (for the purposes of this book you can print on paper). It is, however, possible to set up your own custom sizes.

Task 13.9 Create labels

You will now create name badge labels for those people attending the courses in the previous task. You will therefore be using the same data file.

Method

1   Open a new document. Ensure the Mail Merge toolbar is visible (**View – Toolbars – Mail Merge**).
2   Click on **Main Document Setup** (Figure 13.3).
3   Select **Labels** as the Main Document Type and click **OK**.
4   Select the Label product – **Avery A4 and A5 sizes**. (Figure 13.11)

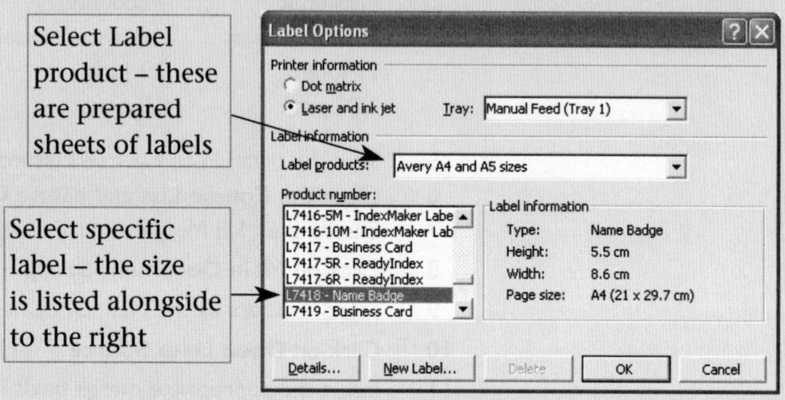

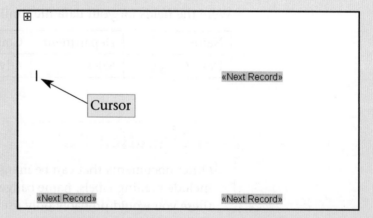

Select Label product – these are prepared sheets of labels

Select specific label – the size is listed alongside to the right

Figure 13.11 Label options

5   Scroll through the Product number list to find **L7418 Name Badge**. (These are in alphabetical then numerical order.) Click **OK**.
6   Click on **Open Data Source**. Locate the **Course List** and click **Open**. The page resembles Figure 13.12.

Cursor

«Next Record»

«Next Record»   «Next Record»

Figure 13.12 Labels – next step

7   Click on **Insert Merge Field** and select **Name**. Click **Insert** and **Close**. Press **Enter** to start a new line.
8   Click on **Insert Merge Field** and select **Department**. Click **Insert** and **Close**.

Hint:

Your field names may differ from those used here depending on how you set up your data file.

9   Click on **Propagate Labels** 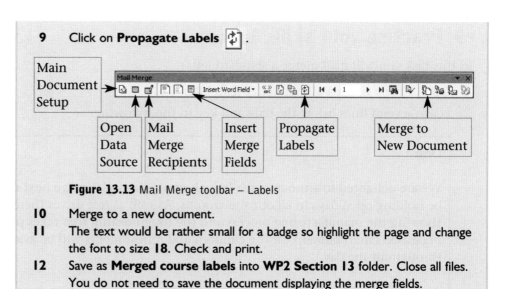.

Main Document Setup

Open Data Source | Mail Merge Recipients | Insert Merge Fields | Propagate Labels | Merge to New Document

Figure 13.13 Mail Merge toolbar – Labels

10   Merge to a new document.
11   The text would be rather small for a badge so highlight the page and change the font to size **18**. Check and print.
12   Save as **Merged course labels** into **WP2 Section 13** folder. Close all files. You do not need to save the document displaying the merge fields.

Hint:

Use Ctrl + A to highlight the entire file.

Information: Mail merge – what can go wrong?

A number of things can go wrong when carrying out a mail merge. For example:

- When inserting the merge fields, you must make sure you leave a space before and after each field or the text will run on continuously.
- If you have inserted a merge field in the wrong place you may get odd results.
- The structure of the data file must suit the data that is to be entered into it, such as addresses containing differing numbers of lines, or you may have problems.
- Data files can be used more than once so make sure you choose the correct data file!

Unexpected results – always merge to a new document before printing to ensure you get what you wanted!

→ Practise your skills 13.1

In this task you will mail merge a standard letter.

1 Open a copy of the Pullman letter template.
2 Leave several lines below the date and key in the following:

Dear *

We are delighted to announce the launch of a new model range next month and will be holding open days in all our showrooms. As well as test drives there will be a film showing the manufacturing process and the tough testing that takes place. We have organised entertainment for the children and refreshments will be available throughout the day.

As a very valued customer we would like to invite you to drop in at any time on 24 June between 10 am and 5 pm at the * showroom. Do please join us. We look forward to seeing you.

Yours sincerely

Your name
Sales Manager

---

3 Save the letter into the **WP2 Section 13** folder as **New model letter**.
4 Set up a mail merge using this letter and the data file **Garage List**. The showroom will be the town where the customers live.
5 Save and print the letter showing the merge fields.
6 Merge the letter to a new document and save it as **Merged new model letters** to the **WP2 Section 13** folder.
7 Print the letters addressed to Mr P Hesketh and Miss L Hamilton.
8 Save and close all files.

→ Practise your skills 13.2

In this task you will create a set of mailing labels addressed to the customers whose details are held in the **Garage List** data file.

1 Create mailing labels using the **Garage List** data file.
2 Use the label product **Avery A4 and A5 sizes**, with product number **C2160 Sticker**.
3 Print the labels. Save as **Garage labels** into the **WP2 Section 13** folder. Close all files.

→ Practise your skills 13.3

In this task you will send a letter to selected recipients.

1 Open a copy of the Pullman letter template.
2 Leave several lines below the date and key in the following:

> Dear *
>
> As you know we are holding an open day on 24 June for the launch of a new model range. This coincides with the appointment of a new Sales Executive at the Christchurch showroom – Ella McKenzie. We are therefore very pleased to be able to offer a bonus pack of extras on any car ordered on the day.
>
> We hope you will take advantage of this special incentive to come along.
>
> Yours sincerely
>
> *Your name*
> Sales Manager

3 Carry out a mail merge using the same **Garage list** data file, inserting the name and address details in the appropriate position, but send this only to those customers living in **Christchurch**.
4 Check, save the merged letters as **Christchurch letters** into the **WP2 Section 13** folder, print and close all files.

→ Check your knowledge

1 What is the most common use for mail merge?
2 What is the purpose of a data file?
3 What types of data might you see in a main document?
4 In Figure 13.14, identify the parts of the data file using these three words:

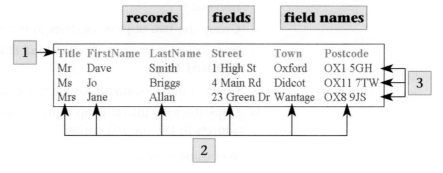

Figure 13.14 A data file

5 What problems can occur when using mail merge?

Practice assignment

You are advised to read all instructions through carefully before starting work, and to check with your tutor, if necessary, to ensure that you have fully understood what is required.

Tasks

A   Logo, template and mail merge
B   Notice
C   Customer Survey
D   Booking Form
E   Announcement

> **Scenario**
>
> You are working for Oakleaf Holidays and have a series of tasks to complete.

Task A – Logo, template and mail merge

In this task you will create a logo, a template and produce a letter to mail merge to potential holidaymakers.

1   Create a new folder called **Oakleaf Holidays**. All files should be saved into this folder.

2   Open a new document and create a Rounded Rectangle 1.5 cm high by 6.5 cm wide and fill with a light green colour.

3   Use WordArt to create the text and fill in a dark green colour.

4   Place this over the rectangle, resizing it and changing the layer order if necessary.

5   Group the two objects together to become one image.

6   Save the document in the **Oakleaf Holidays** folder with the name **Oakleaf Logo**.

7   Create a new document for a letter template.

8   Copy the logo into the top right corner of the page and insert the address in the top left corner:

Woodside Corner

Thorpe Brinton

Norfolk

NF23 8JG

9   Check the letter, adding any names to the dictionary. Insert the date and the filename in the footer.

10 Save the letter as a template file called **Oakleaf Holidays Letter**, print and close.

11 Using a copy of the template, insert today's date and key in the following text. Indicate that a brochure is enclosed:

Dear *

Thank you for your recent enquiry concerning Oakleaf Holidays. We enclose our brochure and hope you will find something to suit your needs. We have also included the up to date availability of our holiday homes, but these change daily and it is always a good idea to check again when you are ready to book.

We look forward to hearing from you again soon. If you have any queries, do please contact us.

Yours sincerely

Your name
Customer Services

---

12 Check the letter and save as **Brochure letter** into the **Oakleaf Holidays** folder.

13 Create the following data file saving it as **Enquiry list** into the new folder.

Title	Firstname	Lastname	Address1	Town	County	Postcode
Mr	Kevin	Batterley	7 Granite Drive	London		EC9 4TR
Mr and Mrs	Len	Porter	St Alban's Way	Leeds		LS16 9KL
Mr	Callum	Connolly	Wordsworth Court	Ellesmere Port	Cheshire	CS16 5FQ
Ms	Jackie	Weyford	14 Palace Gardens	Fallington	S Yorks	LS12 8LP
Mr	Jacques	Dupont	265 Winchester Road	Manchester		M32 8JA

14 Use mail merge to create letters addressed to those listed above.

15 Merge the letters to a new document, check and save as **Merged Enquiry list**.

16 Print a copy of the letter showing the merge fields.

17 Print the letters for Jackie Weyford and Jacques Dupont.

Task B – Notice

1 Open a new document and change the paper size to 21 cm by 21 cm.
2 Set margins of 2.5 cm for top and bottom, and 3 cm for left and right.
3 Key in the following:

Oakleaf Holidays

Information

1. On arrival
   1.1. Check that everything is as you expected.
   1.2. Do you have two sets of keys?
   1.3. Do you have instructions for the use of appliances?
   1.4. Please note evacuation procedures in the case of an emergency.

2. During your stay
   2.1. Contact Reception should any problems arise.
   2.2. Please ensure that all doors and windows are locked when the property is empty.
   2.3. Please park only in the designated spaces.

3. At the end of your stay
   3.1. Please vacate the property by 10.30 am.
   3.2. Hand in keys at Reception.

We hope you enjoy your stay.

---

4 Format item 1 (**On arrival**) as bold with a space after of **12** pt. Create a new style using this paragraph and call it **Main item**. Apply this style to items 2 and 3.

5 Format item 1.1 with a space after of **6** pt. Create a new style using this paragraph and call it **Sub item**. Apply this style to 1.1 etc., 2.1 etc. and 3.1 etc.

6 Change the two headings to larger font sizes, embolden and right align.

7 Place a copy of the logo previously created into the top left corner.

8 Place another copy into the bottom right corner.

9 Add your name to the right of the footer.

10 Check, save as **Notice** and print.

Task C – Customer Survey

1 Set up a new document A5 landscape, with margins of 2 cm all round.

2 Key in the following using checkbox style bullets where appropriate.

Customer Survey

We aim to improve our service to customers and would welcome your feedback.

How did you find out about Oakleaf?
Please tick as appropriate

- ☐ Telephone enquiry
- ☐ Recommendation
- ☐ Magazine
- ☐ Internet
- ☐ TV
- ☐ Radio
- ☐ Previous visit
- ☐ Other

Which of our facilities have you tried during your stay?

- ☐ Harvest Restaurant
- ☐ Dougie's Diner
- ☐ The Gym
- ☐ The Crèche
- ☐ Little Acorns Club
- ☐ Social Club
- ☐ Village Shop

---

3 Insert a continuous section break in front of **How did you find out ...** and centre the text in Section 1.

4 Divide Section 2 into 2 columns.

5 Insert a column break in front of **Which of our facilities ....**

6 Format the two bulleted lists with 1.5 line spacing.

7 Enlarge and embolden the main heading.

8 Copy and paste the logo into the top left corner of the page and reduce it in size.

9 Copy the reduced size logo and place it on the right, ensuring the text still fits on one page.

10 Add your name to the footer.

11 Check the survey, add any new names to the dictionary.

12 Save the file as **Customer Survey**. Load the printer with A5 paper and print.

Task D – Booking Form

1 Open a copy of the **Oakleaf Holidays Letter** template and create the following form.

Booking Form

		Age if under 18
Name of party leader		
Names of party members		
Start Date		
End Date		
Do you require more than one parking space?		Yes/No
Do you require us to supply sheets and towels?		Yes/No
Will you be bringing any pets? If so please give details.		

2 Add your name in the left of the footer. As this will be part of a two-page document, insert the page number and format it to start at page 2.

3 Embolden and enlarge the heading **Booking Form**.

4 Centre the text in the third column.

5 Check and save the document as **Booking form**. Print a copy.

6 Shade the cells in the left-hand column in light green.

7 Merge the cell about parking spaces with the empty cell alongside it.

8 Merge the cell about sheets and towels with the empty cell alongside it.

9 Merge the two empty cells alongside the pets item together.

10 Increase the row heights to use the remainder of the page, ensuring the document still fits on one page.

11 Align all the text within the table cells *vertically*.

12 Save the document and print. If you have access to a colour printer, print in colour, if not, print in black and white.

Task E – Announcement

1 An announcement is needed to send out with the brochures. These will be printed three to an A4 page.

2 Sketch out a layout for the notice using the information given below.

Please note the availability of the following facilities:

Swimming Pools are open from Easter until the end of September.

Sunshine Children's Club is only available during the school holidays.

The crèche is open all year.

This notice replaces any information in our brochure. ☎ 019987 453333

3 The logo should be placed below the text.

4 All the text should be centred and dark green to match the logo.

5 A border should be used around the middle three lines of text with a background fill of light green.

6 Open a new document and create the notice.

7 Copy and paste it to end up with three notices on one page, leaving space between them.

8 Add your name to the left of the header with the filename on the right.

9 Save as **Announcement** and print.

10 Use Find and Replace to replace **Sunshine Children's** with **Little Acorns**.

11 Save as **Announcement 2**.

12 If you have access to a colour printer, print in colour, if not, print in black and white. Close the file.

Assemble all printouts in the correct order and hand in to your tutor.

Solutions

Section 1 Word processing basics
Practise your skills 1.1

The Team

Team members will usually have a mixture of different personal qualities, experience, skills and knowledge and may have been picked for the team for these reasons.

There can be difficulties with team working, especially when team members do not get on, or they do not feel valued or listened to. Sometimes people do not pull their weight and are only too happy to sit back and let others carry them. Occasionally people will only do what they want to do. The team leader and the rest of the team have to cope with these situations. It is essential that everyone knows what is going on, what has to be done and by when.

It is no good people going off in their own direction and failing to meet their targets which will then have a knock-on effect on everybody else and on the project as a whole.

Practise your skills 1.2

WHAT IS A CONSERVATORY?

Once upon a time a conservatory was a glasshouse where delicate plants were placed for the winter. It was also a place where our wealthy Edwardian ancestors grew more exotic flowers and fruits than the British climate would normally allow, for example oranges – hence the term 'orangery' or the French 'orangerie'. Many historic houses such as Blenheim Palace feature an orangery.

The Crystal Palace, built in Hyde Park, London, in 1851 for the Great Exhibition, was a huge conservatory consisting of over a million feet of glass. The building was divided into a series of courts featuring architecture, art, industry and nature. A circus and major concerts were held within the building. Over 6 million visitors, including many from Europe, viewed an exhibition with exhibits from all over the world. When the Great Exhibition finished, the Crystal Palace was moved to South London and rebuilt, where it remained until it was burnt down in 1936.

Check your knowledge

1 A4 portrait.
2 Formatting is changing the appearance of a document, e.g. by changing font, size, alignment, page size and orientation.
3 Editing is changing the content of a document, i.e. the text itself, although it can involve images and other objects.
4 To make sections of text stand out from the rest. It can be used for headings or to draw attention to and emphasise particular words.
5 Text with straight left and right margins.
6 10–12 and left-aligned.

7 When saving a file for the first time you must name it. Subsequently, using Save will save an amended file replacing the original. Save As allows you to give a file a new name or save to a new location, e.g. to a different folder or to a floppy disk.

8 Serif fonts have strokes at the ends of characters. Sans serif fonts do not.

9 Arial and Times New Roman.

10 Check your list against Revise fonts – style and size (page 7).

Section 2 Handling multiple documents and pages

Practise your skills 2.1

Conservatories today

Today's conservatories can make wonderful living spaces. Many people use them as an extra living room rather than a place to put their plants. If you are thinking about a conservatory there are a number of things you should consider.

What do you want to use it for?

Well, you think you want a conservatory but you must ask yourself what you really want to use it for. Is it for storing the plants over the winter? Is it somewhere just to while away summer evenings? Do you want to use it all the year round? Will it be a children's playroom? What furniture do you want to put in there? Is it big enough once the furniture is in there? How are you going to heat it? Do you need power and light? Is it likely to be an all-purpose room?

Practise your skills 2.2

So you want a conservatory?

WHAT IS A CONSERVATORY?

Once upon a time a conservatory was a glasshouse where delicate plants were placed for the winter. It was also a place where our wealthy Edwardian ancestors grew more exotic flowers and fruits than the British climate would normally allow, for example oranges – hence the term 'orangery' or the French 'orangerie'. Many historic houses such as Blenheim Palace feature an orangery.

The Crystal Palace, built in Hyde Park, London, in 1851 for the Great Exhibition, was a huge conservatory consisting of over a million feet of glass. The building was divided into a series of courts featuring architecture, art, industry and nature. A circus and major concerts were held within the building. Over 6 million visitors, including many from Europe, viewed an exhibition with exhibits from all over the world. When the Great Exhibition finished, the Crystal Palace was moved to South London and rebuilt, where it remained until it was burnt down in 1936.

Conservatories today

Today's conservatories can make wonderful living spaces. Many people use them as an extra living room rather than a place to put their plants. If you are thinking about a conservatory there are a number of things you should consider.

What do you want to use it for?

Well, you think you want a conservatory but you must ask yourself what you really want to use it for. Is it for storing the plants over the winter? Is it somewhere just to while away summer evenings? Do you want to use it all the year round? Will it be a children's playroom? What furniture do you want to put in there? Is it big enough once the furniture is in there? How are you going to heat it? Do you need power and light? Is it likely to be an all-purpose room?

Check your knowledge

1 So the reader can follow the sequence in logical order, especially if the order becomes mixed up. They also serve as a point of reference, e.g. 'see page 6'. Page totals show the reader how many pages they should have so they know the document is complete.

2 A placeholder for data that might change in a document, e.g. if the number of pages increases then Page 2 of 4 would become Page 2 of 5.

3 The current date or time might not be what is required. If you open up a file today that you created a few days ago the date will change to today's date.

4 You can see where the pages end, how the headers and footers look and when you have other objects such as images or charts, an impression of how effective and balanced the layout of the finished document will be.

5 A soft page break naturally occurs when the bottom of the page is reached. It will alter automatically as text is added to or deleted from a document. A hard page break is one that is manually inserted and remains in position even when the document is edited.

Section 3 Organising your work

Check your knowledge

1 The hard disk of a standalone computer.

2 A: drive

3 To store related files together so you can find them later.

4 The disk drive light to go out.

5 A copy of a file in case something happens to the original.

Section 4 Bullets and numbering

Practise your skills 4.1

Avalon Sports and Social Club
Meeting to be held on 9th January 2004 at 12.30 pm in the Board Room

Agenda

1. Minutes of the last meeting
2. Treasurer's Report
3. Quiz Evening
4. Summer River Trip
5. Any Other Business

Following the meeting at approximately 1 pm, there will be a buffet lunch to mark the retirement of Bob Dawson and to thank him for all his hard work over the last few years as our Treasurer.

Practise your skills 4.2

Avalon Sports and Social Club
Minutes of the meeting held on 9 January 2004

Present:

Kevin Bailey
Bob Dawson
Emma Hart
Ursula Johannsen
Chi Wai Lee
Peter Marshall
Dan Watson

1. **Minutes of the last meeting – the minutes were agreed.**

2. **Treasurer's Report**
    2.1. Dan has taken over the role of Treasurer and reported that there was £356 in the account.
    2.2. The new signatories had now been set up.

3. **Quiz Evening**
    3.1. Kevin agreed to produce the questions.
    3.2. It was agreed that two bottles of wine would be provided for each team and crisps and nuts would be placed on each table.
    3.3. Ursula volunteered to buy the raffle prizes.

4. **Summer River Trip**
    4.1. The response from staff was good. It was therefore agreed to book this now with a limit of 50 people.
    4.2. Chi Wai volunteered to produce posters and to advertise the event in the newsletter requesting a deposit of £5 per person straight away.

5. **Any Other Business**
    5.1. Bob Dawson's farewell buffet went off very well.
    5.2. All committee members will try to encourage other members of staff to join.
    5.3. The next meeting was arranged for February 13th.

Check your knowledge

1 To display items in a list.
2 This allows more complex numbering for formal documents which have main items and sub-items, e.g. 1, 1.1, 1.2 and 2, 2.1, 2.2 etc.
3 A list of items to be discussed at a meeting, giving the date, time and location.
4 A record of what was discussed at the meeting.
5 Indent it by clicking on the Increase Indent button or pressing the Tab key.

Consolidation 1

Warren First School Activity Day

We are pleased to give you more information about the Activity Day. Each child will take part in two activities. There are four activities to choose from and we hope the children will enjoy the coaching sessions.

The following items will be required for each activity:

1. Badminton
   1.1. Shorts and T Shirt
   1.2. Trainers

2. Football
   2.1. Shorts and T Shirt
   2.2. Football boots

3. Swimming
   3.1. Swimming Trunks/Costume
   3.2. Towel
   3.3. Plastic bag for wet gear

4. Tennis
   4.1. Shorts and T Shirt
   4.2. Trainers

All children will require a packed lunch and plenty of drinks especially if the weather should be particularly warm. Normal start and finish times apply – please make sure the children arrive promptly in the morning.

Please return the slip below to your child's class teacher.

....

Child's name

Choose two out of the four activities listed by ticking the boxes below.

- ❑ Badminton
- ❑ Football
- ❑ Tennis
- ❑ Swimming

Section 5 Paragraph formatting

Practise your skills 5.1

Paragraphs

> This paragraph spreads across the page from the left margin to the right. This paragraph spreads across the page from the left margin to the right. This paragraph spreads across the page from the left margin to the right. This paragraph spreads across the page from the left margin to the right.

> This paragraph is indented 2 cm on the right and the left. This paragraph is indented 2 cm on the right and the left. This paragraph is indented 2 cm on the right and the left. This paragraph is indented 2 cm on the right and the left.

> This paragraph has a hanging indent of 2 cm which means the paragraph is indented 2 cm in from the first line. The first line is 'hanging' away from the rest of the text. This paragraph has a hanging indent of 2 cm which means the paragraph is indented 2 cm in from the first line. The first line is 'hanging' away from the rest of the text.

> This paragraph has a first line indent of 2 cm. This paragraph has a first line indent of 2 cm. This paragraph has a first line indent of 2 cm. This paragraph has a first line indent of 2 cm. This paragraph has a first line indent of 2 cm.

Practise your skills 5.2

So you want a conservatory?

WHAT IS A CONSERVATORY?

Once upon a time a conservatory was a glasshouse where delicate plants were placed for the winter. It was also a place where our wealthy Edwardian ancestors grew more exotic flowers and fruits than the British climate would normally allow, for example oranges – hence the term 'orangery' or the French 'orangerie'. Many historic houses such as Blenheim Palace feature an orangery.

> The Crystal Palace, built in Hyde Park, London, in 1851 for the Great Exhibition, was a huge conservatory consisting of over a million feet of glass. The building was divided into a series of courts featuring architecture, art, industry and nature. A circus and major concerts were held within the building. Over 6 million visitors, including many from Europe, viewed an exhibition with exhibits from all over the world. When the Great Exhibition finished, the Crystal Palace was moved to South London and rebuilt, where it remained until it was burnt down in 1936.

Conservatories today

Today's conservatories can make wonderful living spaces. Many people use them as an extra living room rather than a place to put their plants. If you are thinking about a conservatory there are a number of things you should consider.

What do you want to use it for?

Well, you think you want a conservatory but you must ask yourself what you really want to use it for? Is it for storing the plants over the winter? Is it somewhere just to while away summer evenings? Do you want to use it all the year round? Will it be a children's playroom? What furniture do you want to put in there? Is it big enough once the furniture is in there? How are you going to heat it? Do you need power and light? Is it likely to be an all-purpose room?

Check your knowledge

1 To divide the page at natural points to make it easier to read and to improve the appearance of the page.

2 Ctrl + 2

3 Ctrl + 5

4 To make a paragraph or several paragraphs stand out.

5 True

6
    First line indent
    Hanging indent
    Left indent

Section 6 Checking and proofreading

Practise your skills 6.1

OUTPUT DEVICES

VDUs (Visual Display Units) are available in different sizes measured diagonally across the screen. The screen image is made up of little squares called pixels. The number of pixels affects the clarity of the image and the more pixels, the higher the resolution. Another name for a VDU is a monitor.

Printers – The most common type of printers are the **laser printer** and the **ink-jet**.

The **laser printer** uses a laser beam to build up an image in much the same way as a photocopier and produces a very clear, crisp output. They are more expensive than ink-jets although they have come down considerably in price.

The **ink-jet printer** sprays minute drops of ink onto the paper. Images are built up from dots. These are measured as dots per inch or dpi. They can give high quality output but need good quality paper.

Practise your skills 6.2

A. All staff will receive a pay increase of 2.75% with effect from the 12th of February.
B. The A487 leads from Fishguard to Cardigan via Eglwyswrw.
C. Sven-Goran Erikkson leads the England football team.
D. Steven Spielberg was born on 18 December 1946 in Cincinnati, Ohio
E. Ingredients for Yorkshire pudding are 75 g of plain flour, 1 egg, 75 ml of milk, 50 ml of water plus salt and pepper.

Check your knowledge

1 So that words you use frequently are checked and so that the spellcheck will not stop at those words when it comes across them.

2 They do not check for sense or meaning and only check words that are stored in the dictionary.

3 Refer to bulleted list on page 39.

4 Documents give an impression of an organisation. Inaccuracies can reflect badly on it. Mistyped numbers, dates, etc. can mean lost sales, lost contracts, legal problems. Wrong words might convey the wrong meaning.

5 Layout

Section 7 Tabs

Practise your skills 7.1

Evening Courses

Subject	Weeks	Day	Time
Word Processing Level 1	20	Monday	18.30
Presentation Graphics	10	Tuesday	18.00
Spreadsheets	36	Tuesday	18.30
Word Processing Level 2	20	Wednesday	19.00
Spreadsheets Introduction	10	Wednesday	19.00
Desktop Publishing Level 1	20	Thursday	18.00
Databases	22	Thursday	19.00

Practise your skills 7.2

Course Fees

A list of course fees is given below. If there are any queries concerning these, please refer to Paul Adams, Client Centre Manager, on Extension 7321.

Duration	Fees	Exam Fee
10 week courses	£25.00	£4.50
20 week courses	£50.00	£7.00
22 week courses	£55.00	£7.00
36 week courses	£75.00	£12.50

Practise your skills 7.3

College Canteen

The canteen is open in the evenings between 5.30 and 6.45 pm as a service to those students arriving for their evening class straight from work.

Toasted sandwich	£1.75
Bacon roll	£1.50
Soup and roll	£1.90
Vegetable pasta	£2.60
Jacket potato and salad	£2.10

Tea, coffee and cold drinks are available from the vending machines.

Crisps and chocolate also available from vending machines.

Check your knowledge

1 ⌊ᴸ⌋ Left ⌊ᴶ⌋ Right ⌊⊥⌋ Centre ⌊⊥·⌋ Decimal

2 A type of tab designed to lead your eye across the page making a table easier to read.

3 To arrange numbers that include a decimal point so that all the decimal points line up one below the other.

4 These are tabs set up every 1.27 cm across the page. When a new tab is set, the default tabs to the left of it are cleared.

5 Highlight all the rows of text that you wish to change the tab settings for.

Section 8 Tables

Practise your skills 8.1

The Australian Experience		19 Day Escorted Tour
Day 1	London – Melbourne	City tour 2 days free
Day 4	Melbourne – Adelaide via the Great Ocean Road	3 days Tantanoola Caves Mt Gambier
Day 7	Adelaide – Perth by air	Fremantle Kangaroo Island 1 free day
Day 10	Perth – Alice Springs by air	Gateway to Central Australia Desert Park
Day 12	Alice Springs – Uluru (Ayers Rock)	Outback overnight experience
Day 13	Uluru – Cairns by air	Great Barrier Reef 2 day coastal break
Day 16	Cairns – Sydney by air	Sydney Opera House Harbour Bridge 2 days free
Day 19	Sydney – London	

Practise your skills 8.2

Working with tables

Tick which skills you have achieved.

Skills checklist		Tick here
1	Select a row	
2	Change column width	
3	Change row height	
4	Insert a row	
5	Merge cells vertically	
6	Merge cells horizontally	
7	Change cell alignment	
8	Apply shading	
9	Remove borders	
10	Apply borders	
11	Delete a row/column	
12	Adjust cell margins	
13	Reposition a table	
All skills achieved		

Check your knowledge

1 To set out information into columns and rows.

2 They are a quick, easy and efficient way of setting out information that makes it easy to read.

3 To improve the presentation and to make certain parts of it stand out from the rest.

4 A plan of travel, a tour or journey giving information such as dates, times, and destinations.

Consolidation 2

Summer Fete

The summer fete will take place this year on 14th June. Your help is always appreciated in making this occasion a great success and hopefully we will raise funds towards a new swimming pool cover. Please indicate below if you are able to help

	Setting up	Entrance/Car Park	Manning a stall	Clearing up
10–12				
2–3				
3–4				
4–5				

Name ....

Child's name ....

Class ....

Please return this page to your child's teacher.

Activity Day

We are pleased to give you more information about the Activity Day. Each child will take part in two activities. There are four activities to choose from and we hope the children will enjoy the coaching sessions.

The following items will be required for each activity:

* Badminton
    o Shorts and T Shirt
    o Trainers

* Football
    o Shorts and T Shirt
    o Football boots

* Swimming
    o Swimming Trunks/Costume
    o Towel
    o Plastic bag for wet gear

* Tennis
    o Shorts and T Shirt
    o Trainers

All children will require a packed lunch and plenty of drinks especially if the weather should be particularly warm. Normal start and finish times apply – please make sure the children arrive promptly in the morning.

Please return the slip below to your child's class teacher.

Cut here --

Child's name _____

Choose two out of the four activities listed by ticking the boxes below.

* Badminton

* Football

* Tennis

* Swimming

Summer Fete

The summer fete will take place this year on 14th June. Your help is always appreciated in making this occasion a great success and hopefully we will raise funds towards a new swimming pool cover. Please indicate below if you are able to help

	Setting up	Entrance/Car Park	Manning a stall	Clearing up
10–12				
2–3				
3–4				
4–5				

Name ....

Child's name ....

Class ....

Please return this page to your child's teacher.

Section 9 Templates and business documents
Practise your skills 9.1

To: Jenny Parsons

From: Your name

Date: 1 February 2004

Subject: Absence

I have a dental appointment next Tuesday morning at 10 am and will therefore be absent. I will return as soon as I can and hope that this will not cause an inconvenience.

Practise your skills 9.2

To: Jenny Parsons

From: Your name

Date: 1 February 2004

Subject: Friday Meeting

I can confirm that I am able to attend the meeting on Friday in the Marketing Conference Room.

Practise your skills 9.3

4 Greenmere Place
Anytown
Anywhere
AN1 2EQ

1 February 2004

Miss M Forster
24 Hightown Road
Newtown
Anywhere
AN24 3HT

Dear Megan

I am sorry it has been a while since I last wrote but I have been really busy. If you remember I signed up to do an IT course a while ago and I have been attending college four days a week to gain the City and Guild e-Quals IT User qualification. It has been really enjoyable and I have learnt so much. So far we have done word processing, spreadsheets and presentation graphics, as well as some theory. Soon we will start databases and desktop publishing and I am using the internet and e-mail all the time. Do let me know if you have an e-mail address and I can e-mail you more frequently than writing! I must go now as I do not want to miss the next class.

Best wishes
Yours sincerely

Your name

Check your knowledge

1 It is a file that holds the basic structure of a document, ready for you to use over and over again. It saves time as you do not have to create the document from the beginning every time. It also ensures that a standard layout is always used.

2 A housestyle is a layout that an organisation uses for a document. This might be a letter layout that uses a particular style and a certain font.

3 Where each line starts at the left margin including the salutation and complimentary close.

4 False. If you use the name in the salutation, then close the letter with Yours sincerely. If you do NOT use the name, e.g. Dear Sir, then you use Yours faithfully.

5 Either formal or informal, information or investigation report.

6 An invoice is rather like a bill which states how much money is owed for services provided or goods ordered.

Section 10 Styles

Practise your skills 10.1

Activity Day

We are pleased to give you more information about the Activity Day. Each child will take part in two activities. There are four activities to choose from and we hope the children will enjoy the coaching sessions.

The following items will be required for each activity:

- **Badminton**
  - o Shorts and T Shirt
  - o Trainers

- **Football**
  - o Shorts and T Shirt
  - o Football boots

- **Swimming**
  - o Swimming Trunks/Costume
  - o Towel
  - o Plastic bag for wet gear

- **Tennis**
  - o Shorts and T Shirt
  - o Trainers

All children will require a packed lunch and plenty of drinks especially if the weather should be particularly warm. Normal start and finish times apply – please make sure the children arrive promptly in the morning.

Please return the slip below to your child's class teacher.

Cut here --

Child's name _____

Choose two out of the four activities listed by ticking the boxes below.

- ❑ Badminton

- ❑ Football

- ❑ Tennis

- ❑ Swimming

Summer Fete

The summer fete will take place this year on 14th June. Your help is always appreciated in making this occasion a great success and hopefully we will raise funds towards a new swimming pool cover. Please indicate below if you are able to help

	Setting up	Entrance/Car Park	Manning a stall	Clearing up
10-12				
2-3				
3-4				
4-5				

Name ....

Child's name ....

Class ....

Please return this page to your child's teacher.

Practise your skills 10.2

Avalon Sports and Social Club
Minutes of the meeting held on 9 January 2004

Present:

Kevin Bailey
Bob Dawson
Emma Hart
Ursula Johannsen
Chi Wai Lee
Peter Marshall
Dan Watson

1. **Minutes of the last meeting – the minutes were agreed.**

2. **Treasurer's Report**
   2.1. Dan has taken over the role of Treasurer and reported that there was £356 in the account.
   2.2. The new signatories had now been set up.

3. **Quiz Evening**
   3.1. Kevin agreed to produce the questions.
   3.2. It was agreed that two bottles of wine would be provided for each team and crisps and nuts would be placed on each table.
   3.3. Ursula volunteered to buy the raffle prizes.

4. **Summer River Trip**
   4.1. The response from staff was good. It was therefore agreed to book this now with a limit of 50 people.
   4.2. Chi Wai volunteered to produce posters and to advertise the event in the newsletter requesting a deposit of £5 per person straight away.

5. **Any Other Business**
   5.1. Bob Dawson's farewell buffet went off very well.
   5.2. All committee members will try to encourage other members of staff to join.
   5.3. The next meeting was arranged for February 13th.

Check your knowledge

1 They are a quick way of applying formats to text and ensuring consistency throughout a document. Change the style once and every piece of text tagged with that style will change automatically.

2 Click into the text to which the style is to be applied, or highlight it if there are several paragraphs, then click on the drop down list of styles, selecting the required style.

3 Format text and then click into the Style box, keying in a name for the style.

4 Normal style.

Section 11 Graphics and charts

Practise your skills 11.1

Greentops Nursery

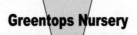

For all your gardening needs
Monday – Friday 8 am – 6 pm
Saturday 8 am – 6 pm
Sunday 9 am – 5 pm
Langley Road, Bixford

Greentops Nursery

Greentops Nursery

For all your gardening needs

Monday – Friday 8 am – 6 pm

Saturday 8 am – 6 pm

Sunday 9 am – 5 pm

Langley Road, Bixford

Greentops Nursery

Boxford Conservatories coming to your area soon

We are a family business established in 1986

- Great prices
- A variety of styles and finishes
- Delivery on time
- Experienced craftsmen fitters
- Satisfaction guaranteed or your money back

 **If you are thinking of installing a conservatory in the near future call us now to see what we can do for you. You will be amazed at our prices and the choice of styles – there is sure to be something to fit your budget.**

Call now on 01997 255643

Check your knowledge

1 If you check this feature when changing the size or scale of an object, it will keep it in its original proportion.

2 An **inline** object is positioned directly in the text and is fixed at the point in the text it is placed. A **floating** object has text wrapping applied to it and can be positioned anywhere on the page.

3 Anywhere around the end of the page or in the corners, to ensure the text remains easy to read.

4 Are they necessary? Do they improve the document? Are the graphics used relevant to the document? Are they in the right place, i.e. with the text that relates to them? Do they look right? Sometimes adjusting the position or size a little can make all the difference to the way the text wraps around them.

5 Objects can be grouped together to make them easier to manipulate, as you only have to handle one object rather than several. You can also ungroup objects if you should want to edit them in some way.

6 To display numbers in a pictorial way, making them easier to understand at a glance.

Consolidation 3

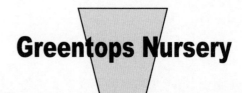

Greentops Nursery

Langley Road
Bixford
BX7 9RD

Tel: **019966 654777**

22 February 2004

Mr A Shafi
GroFasta Products
Anytown
Anywhere
AN1 5WH

Dear Mr Shafi

GroFasta Fertilizer

It is now three months since we agreed to stock your new product Grofasta at special discount rates and as agreed, we have carried out checks to see how your product has sold over the last six weeks. This is best illustrated by the chart below.

Sales of GroFasta showing sales in hundreds

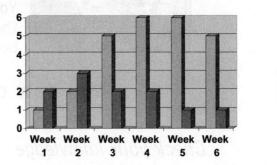

As you can see sales increased significantly following your national advertising campaign, whilst your main competitor's went down. I enclose a further breakdown of the daily figures. I hope this information will be useful to you and I look forward to negotiating continued discount rates with you.

Yours sincerely

Your name
Manager

Enc

Section 12 Document editing and formatting

Practise your skills 12.1

PROJECT TEAMS

Team Working

A group of people working well together will usually complete a task quicker than one person on their own. There is a well-known saying - many hands make light work - and another similar one - two heads are better than one. However, it is not quite as simple as that as successful team working depends on a number of factors.

If a group of people are put together as a team to work on a project, they may have no idea how to begin. In a small team there may be no appointed leader, but often a natural leader will emerge. If there is a leader the team will look to the leader to get things started. As the team members begin to work together, progress can be made. If they do not co-operate and work well together then progress will be difficult. Problems can occur if everyone does not pull their weight or if some people feel their contribution is not valued by others.

The Planning Stage

Before a project can begin, this is what should be considered:

- What is required?
- When does it have to be completed?
- What resources are needed, e.g. materials, equipment, finance?
- What are the main tasks?
- Can some tasks be carried out at the same time or can they overlap?
- Which tasks have to be finished before others can begin?
- When does each separate task have to be completed?
- Who is responsible for what?
- Is the <u>best</u> use made of each team member's individual qualities, experience, knowledge and skills?

REMEMBER - make sure everyone knows what is going on. A winning team works together.

Practise your skills 12.2

The Board of Directors of AT have recognised that changes must be made at Group Management Team level. Three years ago AT was a flourishing business in all respects and it is our wish that this should continue over the coming year.

The review of AT's trading results will be detailed next week by Mark Cairns at the conference at the Sands Hotel in Handsworth.

This year has been a difficult one for AT since so many of our activities depend upon the economic climate in other countries. AT's sales in the USA fell whilst those in Europe maintained a marked growth pattern. AT's future in the USA will be the subject of a Study to be announced at a later date.

An announcement on the new plant site for AT in the UK will be made at next month's Board Meeting, and this will allow further development of AT's interests in the home market.

Check your knowledge

1 A break which creates a new section but continues on the current page.

2 Next page section breaks start a new page and create a new section at the same time.

3 Highlight the text as required and click on the Columns button. Drag to highlight the required number of columns.

4 Word moves any text that follows to the top of the next column.

5 A feature that allows you to replace one word with another throughout a document.

6 Match whole words only.

Section 13 mail merge

Practise your skills 13.1

Barrington Park
Upper Causeway
Oxon
OX21 4PH
Tel: 01637 224475 Fax: 01637 224476
www.pullmanplc.co.uk
enquiries@pullmanplc.co.uk

today's date

«Title» «Initial» «Lastname»
«Address1»
«Address2»
«Town»
«County»
«Postcode»

Dear «Title» «Lastname»

We are delighted to announce the launch of a new model range next month and will be holding open days in all our showrooms. As well as test drives there will be a film showing the manufacturing process and the tough testing that takes place. We have organised entertainment for the children and refreshments will be available throughout the day.

As a very valued customer we would like to invite you to drop in on 24 June at any time between 10 am and 5 pm at the «Town» showroom. Do please join us. We look forward to seeing you.

Yours sincerely

Your name
Sales Manager

Pullman plc

Barrington Park
Upper Causeway
Oxon
OX21 4PH
Tel: 01637 224475 Fax: 01637 224476
www.pullmanplc.co.uk
enquiries@pullmanplc.co.uk

today's date

Mr P Hesketh
24 The Moors
Poole
Dorset
BH23 5TW

Dear Mr Hesketh

We are delighted to announce the launch of a new model range next month and will be holding open days in all our showrooms. As well as test drives there will be a film showing the manufacturing process and the tough testing that takes place. We have organised entertainment for the children and refreshments will be available throughout the day.

As a very valued customer we would like to invite you to drop in on 24 June at any time between 10 am and 5 pm at the Poole showroom. Do please join us. We look forward to seeing you.

Yours sincerely

Your name
Sales Manager

Practise your skills 13.2

Mr P Hesketh	Mrs L Rana	Mr and Mrs G Elliot
24 The Moors	78 Castle View	Albany House
Poole	Meadowside	129 Wanstead Road
Dorset	Christchurch	Bournemouth
BH23 5TW	Dorset	Dorset
	BH10 7KH	BH11 7WZ
Ms J Connor	Mr and Mrs I Paulik	Miss L Hamilton
Flat 4	1 Cholwell Drive	9 Perivale View
32 Holly Drive	Bournemouth	Southampton
Christchurch	Dorset	Hants
Dorset	BH11 2QS	SO22 9FR
BH10 9KL		

Pullman plc

Barrington Park
Upper Causeway
Oxon
OX21 4PH
Tel: 01637 224475 Fax: 01637 224476
www.pullmanplc.co.uk
enquiries@pullmanplc.co.uk

Today's date

Mrs L Rana
78 Castle View
Meadowside
Christchurch
Dorset
BH10 7KH

Dear Mrs Rana

As you know we are holding an open day on 24 June for the launch of a new model range. This coincides with the appointment of a new Sales Executive at the Christchurch showroom – Ella McKenzie. We are therefore very pleased to be able to offer a bonus pack of extras on any car ordered on the day.

We hope you will take advantage of this special incentive to come along.

Yours sincerely

Your name
Sales Manager

Check your knowledge

1 For producing individual letters to send out to a list of people.

2 It holds the variable information that will be merged with the main document to make each document different, e.g. a list of names and addresses.

3 If it is a letter, it will hold text that will be the same for each letter as well as fields where the variable information will go. If it is a label, then only field names.

4 1 – field names, 2 – fields, 3 – records

5 See paragraph entitled 'Mail merge – what can go wrong?' on page 117.

Practice assignment
Task A

Woodside Corner
Thorpe Brinton
Norfolk
NF23 8JG

Oakleaf Holidays

Today's date

«Title» «Firstname» «Lastname»
«Address1»
«Town»
«County»
«Postcode»

Dear «Title» «Lastname»

Thank you for your recent enquiry concerning Oakleaf Holidays. We enclose our brochure and hope you will find something to suit your needs. We have also included the up to date availability of our holiday homes, but these change daily and it is always a good idea to check again when you are ready to book.

We look forward to hearing from you again soon. If you have any queries, do please contact us.

Yours sincerely

Your name
Customer Services

Encs

Woodside Corner
Thorpe Brinton
Norfolk
NF23 8JG

Oakleaf Holidays

Today's date

Ms Jackie Weyford
14 Palace Gardens
Fallington
S Yorks
LS12 8LP

Dear Ms Weyford

Thank you for your recent enquiry concerning Oakleaf Holidays. We enclose our brochure and hope you will find something to suit your needs. We have also included the up to date availability of our holiday homes, but these change daily and it is always a good idea to check again when you are ready to book.

We look forward to hearing from you again soon. If you have any queries, do please contact us.

Yours sincerely

Your name
Customer Services

Encs

Task B

Oakleaf Holidays

Information

1. **On arrival**

    1.1. Check that everything is as you expected.

    1.2. Do you have two sets of keys?

    1.3. Do you have instructions for the use of appliances?

    1.4. Please note evacuation procedures in the case of an emergency

2. **During your stay**

    2.1. Contact Reception should any problems arise.

    2.2. Please ensure that all doors and windows are locked when the property is empty.

    2.3. Please park only in the designated spaces.

3. **At the end of your stay**

    3.1. Please vacate the property by 10.30 am.

    3.2. Hand in keys at Reception.

We hope you enjoy your stay.

Your name

Task C

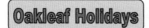

Customer Survey

We aim to improve our service to customers and would welcome your feedback.

How did you find out about Oakleaf?
Please tick as appropriate

- ❑ Telephone enquiry
- ❑ Recommendation
- ❑ Magazine
- ❑ Internet
- ❑ TV
- ❑ Radio
- ❑ Previous visit
- ❑ Other

Which of our facilities have you tried during your stay?

- ❑ Harvest Restaurant
- ❑ Dougie's Diner
- ❑ The Gym
- ❑ The Crèche
- ❑ Little Acorns Club
- ❑ Social Club
- ❑ Village Shop

Your name

Task D

Woodside Corner
Thorpe Brinton
Norfolk
NF23 8JG

Booking Form

		Age if under 18
Name of party leader		
Names of party members		
Start Date		
End Date		
Do you require more than one parking spaces?		Yes/No
Do you require us to supply sheets and towels?		Yes/No
Will you be bringing any pets? If so please give details.		

Your name   2

Task E

Your name

Please note the availability of the following facilities:

> Swimming Pools are open from Easter until the end of September.
> Little Acorns Club is only available during the school holidays.
> The crèche is open all year.

This notice replaces any information in our brochure. ☎ 019987 453333

Please note the availability of the following facilities:

> Swimming Pools are open from Easter until the end of September.
> Little Acorns Club is only available during the school holidays.
> The crèche is open all year.

This notice replaces any information in our brochure. ☎ 019987 453333

Oakleaf Holidays

Please note the availability of the following facilities:

> Swimming Pools are open from Easter until the end of September.
> Little Acorns Club is only available during the school holidays.
> The crèche is open all year.

This notice replaces any information in our brochure. ☎ 019987 453333

Oakleaf Holidays

Outcomes matching guide

Outcome 1 Plan and prepare to produce new documents
Practical activities

1	Produce draft layouts for different types of document	Sections 8, 9, 11, 12, 13
2	Plan the production of documents and the facilities required: mail merge, templates	Sections 9, 13
3	Sketch suitable positioning and appearance of required text and graphics	Sections 8, 9, 13
4	Check the required data is available	Sections 11, 12, 13

Underpinning knowledge

1	Identify common types of documents	Sections 8, 9, 11, 13
2	Describe how common word processing facilities (e.g. mail merge, templates, tables and styles) can be used to produce documents efficiently	Sections 8, 9, 10, 13
3	Identify the main paper sizes and state their typical uses	Section 1
4	State how different styles and sizes of fonts can affect the appearance of a document	Section 1
5	State the purpose of text enhancement and when it should be used	Section 1
6	Identify common methods used to structure text	Sections 1, 4, 5, 7, 8, 12
7	State how the use and positioning of graphics can be used to improve the appearance of a document	Section 11

Outcome 2 Produce new documents
Practical activities

1	Start the word processing software with new blank documents or templates where suitable	Section 9
2	Use templates to produce documents, including business letters, memos and reports as required	Sections 9, 10, 11, 13
3	Set up page layout for planned documents	All sections
4	Create headers and footers for the document, with suitable content	All sections from 2 onwards
5	Input required text with suitable formatting: • Special symbols • Different alignments • Enhancement • Tabulation • Font size and style and horizontal spacing • Paragraphs and indentation • Bulleted and numbered lists	Section 11 Section 1 Section 1 Sections 7, 8 Section 11 Section 5 Section 4
6	Insert section, column and page breaks as required	Sections 2, 12
7	Select and insert objects in suitable positions: • Date, time and filename fields • Files • Charts and graphics	Section 2 Section 12 Section 11

8	Adjust the size/scale of inserted objects	Section 11
9	Copy and paste text from existing documents into new documents	Section 2
10	Insert tables into documents	Section 8
11	Format tables to achieve suitable presentation	Section 8
12	Insert automatic page numberings	Section 2

Underpinning knowledge

1	Identify suitable uses for text enhancement and lines, borders and shading in documents	Sections 1, 5, 8
2	Identify the main purposes of using headers and footers, and their contents	Section 2
3	Describe the reasons for using graphic representation of data in documents	Section 11
4	Describe the reasons for using date, time and filename fields, and their limitations	Section 2
5	Describe suitable uses for tables in word processed documents	Sections 7, 8
6	State the difference between hard and soft page breaks	Section 2
7	Identify when hard page breaks should be used	Section 2
8	State the importance of page numbering and page totals	Section 2

Outcome 3 Produce new documents using mail merge facilities
Practical activities

1	Plan suitable structures for data files	Section 13
2	Create data files and input the required data	Section 13
3	Create main documents to be used in merges, and link them to data files	Section 13
4	Insert required merge fields into main documents	Section 13
5	Merge documents and preview the results	Section 13
6	Produce merged output to screen, storage and printer	Section 13

Underpinning knowledge

1	Describe common uses of mail merge facilities in word processing	Section 13
2	Identify the types of data that should be in the main document of mail merges	Section 13
3	Describe the purpose of data files used in mail merges	Section 13
4	Describe how data files are structured	Section 13
5	Describe problems that might occur during mail merge operations	Section 13

Outcome 4 Edit existing documents
Practical activities

1	Open existing documents for editing from hard disk and floppy disk	All sections
2	Check existing page layouts and change as required	All sections from 2 onwards

3	Edit characters, text blocks and graphics in existing documents	Sections 1, 11
4	Check existing text formats and change as required	All sections
5	Select and use styles to apply multiple changes to text formatting	Section 10
6	Create and apply new styles to achieve suitable presentation	Section 10
7	Modify the positioning and formatting of objects in a document (charts and graphics)	Section 11
8	Modify section, column and page breaks as required	Sections 2, 12
9	Check page numbering and page totals and modify as required	Section 2

Underpinning knowledge

1	Describe the advantages of using styles	Section 10
2	Describe the reasons for grouping and ungrouping objects	Section 11

Outcome 5 Check produced documents
Practical activities

1	Use a spellchecker on part and whole documents, and change text as required	Section 6
2	Add new words to the spellchecker as required	Section 6
3	Proofread documents to check accuracy, correctness and meaning	Section 6
4	Use Find and Replace to make corrections to whole documents	Section 12
5	Use print preview to check the layout of the finished document and change as required	Section 2

Underpinning knowledge

1	Explain why it is necessary to add new words to the dictionary of a spellchecker	Section 6
2	Identify the limitations of automated spellcheckers	Section 6
3	State the importance of checking documents for accuracy, correctness and meaning	Section 6
4	State the importance of checking the layout of the finished document in a wysiwyg display such as print preview	Sections 2, 6

Outcome 6 Save and print documents
Practical activities

1	Save documents with suitable filenames in specified locations	All sections
2	Save page layouts as templates	Section 9
3	Make copies of a document giving them new name using Save As	Section 1
4	Add paper to the printer as necessary	Section 1
5	Print check and preview documents	Section 2
6	Check printed output for accuracy and layout	Section 6
7	Close finished documents and the word processing software	All sections

Underpinning knowledge

1	State the difference between Save and Save As and when each should be used	Section 1
2	Describe the main purposes of templates	Section 9

Quick reference guide

Action	Button	Menu	Keyboard
Bold	**B**	Format – Font	Ctrl + B
Borders	⊞	Format – Borders and Shading	
Bring to front (graphics)	Draw ▾ – Order – Bring to Front		
Bullets	≣	Format – Bullets and Numbering – Bulleted	
Cancel			Esc
Centre align	≣	Format – Paragraph – Indents and Spacing	Ctrl + E
Character spacing		Format – Font – Character spacing	
Chart		Insert – Object – Microsoft Graph	
Close or Exit		File – Close or Exit	Alt + F4
Column break		Insert – Break – Column Break	
Columns	▥	Format – Columns	
Copy	📄	Edit – Copy	Ctrl + C
Cut	✂	Edit – Cut	Ctrl + X
Decrease indent	⮜≣	Format – Paragraph – Indents and Spacing	
Demote	⮞≣	Format – Paragraph – Indents and Spacing	
Drawing toolbar		View – Toolbars – Drawing	
End of line			End
Exit or Close		File – Close or Exit	Alt + F4
Find		Edit – Find	Ctrl + F
First line indent		Format – Paragraph – Special	
Font	Times New Roman ▾	Format – Font – Font	
Font size	12 ▾	Format – Font – Font	
Group objects	Draw ▾ on Drawing toolbar then Group		

Hanging indent		Format – Paragraph – Indents and Spacing – Special	
Header/Footer		View – Header and Footer	
Increase indent	![icon]	Format – Paragraph – Indents and Spacing	Ctrl + M
Insert clip art	![icon] From Drawing toolbar	Insert – Picture – ClipArt	
Italics	*I*	Format – Font – Font	Ctrl + I
Justify	![icon]	Format – Paragraph – Indents and Spacing	Ctrl + J
Left align	![icon]	Format – Paragraph – Indents and Spacing	Ctrl + L
Line spacing		Format – Paragraph – Indents and Spacing – Line Spacing	Single – Ctrl + 1 $1\frac{1}{2}$ – Ctrl + 5 Double – Ctrl + 2
Margins		File – Page Setup – Margins	
New file	![icon]	File – New	Ctrl + N
Normal view	![icon] left above status bar	View – Normal	
Numbering	![icon]	Format – Bullets and Numbering – Numbered	
Open file	![icon]	File – Open	Ctrl + O
Order (graphics)	Draw ▾ on Drawing toolbar – Order		
Page break		Insert – Break – Page Break	Ctrl + Return
Page number		Insert – Page Numbers or View – Header and Footer	
Page setup		File – Page Setup	
Paper size/orientation		File – Page Setup – Paper Size	
Paste	![icon]	Edit – Paste	Ctrl + V
Print	![icon]	File – Print	Ctrl + P
Print layout view	![icon] left above status bar	View – Print Layout	
Print preview	![icon]	File – Print Preview	Ctrl + F2
Promote	![icon]	Format – Paragraph – Indents and Spacing	Ctrl + M

Redo	⟳		
Replace		Edit – Replace	Ctrl + H
Right align	≣	Format – Paragraph – Indents and Spacing	Ctrl + R
Ruler		View – Ruler	
Save	💾	File – Save	Ctrl + S
Save As		File – Save As	F12
Search		Edit – Find	Ctrl + F
Section break		Insert – Break – Continuous (or Next page) Section Break	
Select all		Edit – Select All	Ctrl + A
Send to back (graphics)	Draw ▾ on Drawing toolbar – Order – Send to Back		
Shading		Format – Borders and Shading	
Show/Hide	¶		
Shrink to fit	🔍 and then 📑		
Space before/after a paragraph		Format – Paragraph – Spacing Before or After	
Spellcheck	✓ABC	Tools – Spelling and Grammar	F7
Start of line			Home
Subscript/Superscript		Format – Font – Font tab, select as required	
Symbol		Insert – Symbol	
Switch between files		Window – select file	
Table	▦	Table – Insert – Table	
Tabs	⌞ Select tab type and click on ruler	Format – Tabs	
Text wrapping	▣	View – Toolbars – Picture or Format – Object – Layout	
Underline	U	Format – Font – Font	Ctrl + U
Undo	↶	Edit – Undo	Ctrl + Z
Ungroup objects	Draw ▾ on Drawing toolbar then Ungroup		
WordArt	◢ on Drawing toolbar	Insert – Picture – WordArt	

Select text

To select:	Method
One word	Double click on word (also selects the following space)
Several words	Press and drag the I-beam across several words and release
A line	Click alongside line in left margin (mouse pointer changes to an arrow pointing right)
A paragraph	Double click alongside paragraph in left margin
A sentence	Hold down **Ctrl**. Click anywhere in sentence
Whole document	Hold down **Ctrl** and click in left margin **OR** choose Select All from Edit menu
A block of text	Click cursor at start point, hold down **Shift**. Click cursor at end point
To deselect	Click anywhere off the text

Right mouse button

Clicking the right mouse button provides menu options depending on what you are doing at the time, e.g. when right clicked in a normal paragraph you have Cut, Copy, Paste, etc. When right clicked in a table you have Table options.

Drawing toolbar

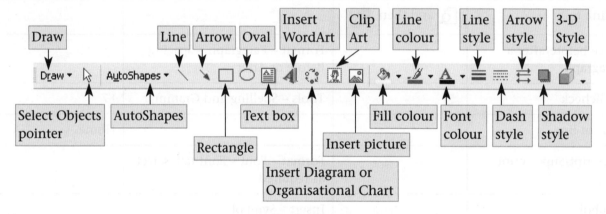

Help

For Help at any time, click on the **Help** menu and select **Microsoft Word Help**. The Office Assistant appears. Type in a question and click on **Search** for a list of possible solutions from which to choose. To turn off the Office Assistant, select **Hide Office Assistant** from the **Help** menu.